Top Tips
for Contented Babies
and Toddlers

Gina Ford

Vermilion
LONDON

First published in the United Kingdom in 2005 by Vermilion

This edition published in the United Kingdom 2005 h
by Vermilion, an imprint of Ebury Publishing
Random House UK, UK.

Random House · 20 Vauxhall Bridge Road · London SW1V 2SA

Random House Australia (Pty) Limited
20 Alfred Street · Milsons Point · Sydney · New South Wales 2061 · Australia

Random House New Zealand Limited
18 Poland Road · Glenfield · Auckland 10 · New Zealand

Random House (Pty) Limited
Isle of Houghton · Corner of Boundary Road & Carse O'Gowrie,
Houghton 2198 · South Africa

Random House UK Limited Reg. No. 954009
www.randomhouse.co.uk

Papers used by Vermilion are natural, recyclable products made from
wood grown in sustainable forests.

A CIP catalogue record for this book is available from the British Library

ISBN: 0091912725
ISBN: 97800919212727 (from Jan 2007)

Text design by Lovelock & Co.
Printed and bound in Great Britain by Mackays of Chatham plc · Chatham · Kent

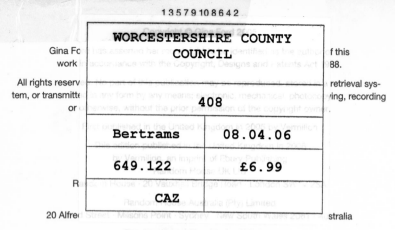

Contents

Introduction

I wrote *The Contented Little Baby Book* to pass on what I'd learnt during my career as a maternity nurse and child-care consultant to parents who were desperate for a successful way to look after their babies. Many new parents, I discovered, were finding demand-feeding and sleepless nights distressing and destructive to family life, and needed help. I wanted to answer that need and pass on what I'd come to believe in over the years. Letters and calls from thousands of parents have told me how much my methods have helped them when they have been at breaking point. Of course, my approach might not suit everyone, but I know it can help relieve the stress and confusion of early parenthood, and has done so for many mothers and fathers.

My experience of babies and children is based on a career giving hands-on, practical advice, and seeing at first hand how a contented little baby and child greatly enhances the enjoyment of their early years for the whole family. I developed my methods through living with families in a variety of homes and helping them get to grips with parenthood. My routines are based on a firm belief that, with a sensible, practical approach, those early years need not cause the many sleepless nights and all-round exhaustion that beset some parents. Those who are already familiar with my methods will know that I am a great believer in consistent routines for babies and children, and I cover many of the topics in *Top Tips* in more detail in my other books. This book is a concise insight into my methods, covering all the areas of raising a baby and child, including sleeping, feeding, weaning and potty training. It's a quick, practical guide for those mothers and fathers who would like to know what makes a contented little baby and child. I hope it provides some help and inspiration for those parents who need it.

Gina Ford

Note: For simplicity's sake, the baby or child is referred to throughout as 'he'.

1
Sleeping

Sleeping is one of the main preoccupations of new parents. How much does the baby sleep? How long are the sleeps? How often does he wake during the night? Nothing can prepare you for the intense work that your new baby will entail, and for the exhaustion that can follow from constantly interrupted nights. The sooner a baby is able to sleep through the night, the better for the whole family, and I believe that with persistence and careful planning, there is no reason why this shouldn't be possible from a young age. Sleep deprivation in children is a serious problem these days, and starting healthy habits young is, I think, one of the ways to solve it.

Nothing in my methods involves depriving a baby of anything; rather, they concentrate on learning to anticipate a baby's needs long before the crying and sleepless nights set in. If a baby has got into a routine of excessive night-time waking, it is possible to guide him gradually into better sleeping habits. The tips that follow are designed to help parents quickly and practically. (You can find an in-depth discussion of sleep in *The Complete Sleep Guide for Contented Babies and Toddlers*.)

Parents always ask me what it is I do with my babies in the night to get them to sleep so well. The answer is always the same: very little. I try to establish a routine in the early weeks and make sure of some simple things: that the baby is sleeping neither too much nor too little during the day; that he is not overstimulated; that he does not learn to depend on sleep associations, such as rocking, feeding and being walked about; that he is fed enough in the day and at the right times so that he does not need to wake in the night.

BASIC GOOD SLEEP PRACTICE

There are several things you can do to make sure that you have the best environment to encourage good sleep habits in your child.

✿ Most importantly, a well-fitted black-out blind to ensure complete darkness in the nursery.

✿ It is important for a baby to have his own space for sleep times. Whether it is in a nursery or in a corner of your bedroom, establish a place designated for sleep, away from the hustle and bustle of everyday activities. This helps the baby to relax and be happy in his own company.

- The ideal room temperature is 18°C (64°F). An overheated room is not only a contributor to cot death, but can dry the mucous membranes of the nose and make a baby very uncomfortable.

- Keep the cot or bed away from the radiator, window or outside wall.

- Bedding and clothing should be 100 per cent cotton. Quilts, bumpers and pillows should be avoided as they can cause overheating. If you are swaddling during the first month, reduce the layers of bedding accordingly.

- Keep the bedding clean and the room well aired and regularly vacuumed. Also vacuum the mattress, which must conform to British safety standards (BS1877 and BS7177), be clean, firm and fit properly.

- Simple cotton sleepwear is best; avoid buttons at the back, collars and fancy ribbons, and remove any irritations, such as loose threads or stiff labels. The best design is a sleepsuit that fastens under the legs.

- During hot weather pull blinds down during the day to keep the room cool, or use a fan, taking care that it doesn't blow directly on the baby or sit within reach of a child. Make sure the baby is not overcovered; very little is needed to keep a baby warm in excessively hot weather.

- The best way to check if a baby is too hot or too cold is to feel the back of his neck. Having done that, adjust clothes and bedding accordingly.

- Babies can sometimes wake themselves up by twitching or jerking (this is called the Moro reflex), and in the early weeks swaddling and firm tucking in can help to overcome this.

- Toys, activity centres and mobiles should all be removed when a baby is asleep. Not only can they wake the baby up if he moves on to them, but they can be confusing. Establishing the difference between sleep times and wake times is one of the keys to helping a baby sleep well. Later, toddlers can take a favourite toy to bed with them.

- I don't encourage bed sharing for two main reasons: the first is safety and the second is sleep association. Experts are coming to the opinion that the risk of suffocation is greater when a baby sleeps with adults, and I advise that a Moses basket next to the bed or a cot with a detachable side is the safest way to have the baby near you. Sleep associations can lead to a baby being unable to sleep alone, and dependent on the presence of parents.

- The safest position for a baby to sleep in is on his back, and firm tucking in will help him feel comfortable and secure in this position.

- Never allow your baby to fall asleep in the house in his outdoor things; always remove hats, mitts and coats.

- Never allow anyone to smoke near your baby or in the baby's room.

- Ensure that toddlers, young children and animals are kept out of the nursery.

- If you are feeling at breaking point, it is better to put the baby in his cot for five or 10 minutes while you recharge than to risk falling asleep with him on the sofa.

Darkness and sleeping

In my opinion, the key to night-time sleeping is daytime sleeping, and absolutely vital to both is darkness. Here I differ from many other experts, but in my experience, teaching the baby the difference between time asleep and time awake is best achieved by making sure that in the early days he is put to sleep in a dark room for most of his naps. Research has proved that the pineal gland produces a natural substance called melatonin, which works as a sedative. The release of this hormone is stimulated by darkness and prepares the body for sleep.

All babies come into a light sleep after 45 minutes, and even the smallest amount of light can be enough to prevent them from settling themselves back to sleep.

✿ Make sure the room is in complete darkness by using black-out blinds and eliminating chinks of light above and below the curtains.

✿ Make sure that the door is closed and there is quiet.

WHY IS MY BABY NOT SLEEPING?

These are the main causes for a healthy baby under one year of age waking excessively during the night.

Hunger. A baby who has not fed enough during the day will be harder to settle, and will be likely to wake at night needing more.

Not feeding enough at each feed. In the early days a baby can need at least 25 minutes on one breast. If the baby's milk feeds are reduced too quickly when solids are introduced, he will begin to wake in the night genuinely needing a milk feed.

Sleeping too much during the day. A baby will settle to sleep only if he is tired and ready to sleep.

Not sleeping enough during the day. Overtiredness can make a baby fight sleep.

Overstimulation. A baby needs a proper period of quietness and wind-down to prepare for allowing himself to go to sleep.

Waking himself up. Babies under six weeks have a very strong Moro reflex, and can wake themselves several times a night by suddenly jerking. To avoid this, swaddle the baby in a lightweight stretch cotton sheet, or tuck in firmly.

Getting cold. Older babies often kick their covers off and become cold, or can get their legs caught between the bars of the cot. A sleeping bag will prevent this.

Wrong sleep associations. If the baby is used to being fed, rocked or given a dummy to get to sleep, he will need the same assistance to resettle himself in the night when he wakes.

Outside disturbance. Parents who leave the nursery door open or leave a night-light on are more likely to be woken several times a night.

The first things to look at in every case are the most important: feeding and daytime sleeping.

Feeding

Your baby could be waking up simply because he is hungry. Nearly 80 per cent of the sleeping problems that I have to deal with between the ages of six months and one year are caused by the feeding patterns not being right. I often speak to parents of older babies who are still waking and feeding two or three times a night simply because they are not getting enough to eat during the day. By the time they reach nine months, a vicious circle has been established. The baby will not eat enough during the day because he is having milk during the night, and he will not sleep at night without the milk because he has not had enough to eat during the day. Obviously, young babies must never be made to wait for food when they are hungry, but it is also important that you understand your child's nutritional needs and that you structure his daily intake according to age.

Tips to structure food and sleep

✿ To avoid excessive night feeding, a baby under six weeks needs to have at least six feeds between 7am and 11pm. A baby aged between six weeks and six months needs four to five feeds between 7am and 11pm.

✿ It is also important that a baby gets enough to eat at each feed.

In the early days most babies need a minimum of 25 minutes on the first breast, and a baby over 3.5kg (8lb) in weight should be offered the second breast.

* A formula-fed baby needs 75–90ml (2½–3oz) of milk per pound of his body weight each day, divided into the number of feeds he is having. Breast-fed babies will be more likely to wake up several times a night if they do not get enough to eat at the 10pm feed and may need a top-up after this feed.

* Babies over 4kg (9lb) in weight should be able to sleep one longer spell during the night provided they are gaining 180–250g (6–8oz) each week and are taking most of their daily milk allowance between 7am and 11pm.

* How long a baby will continue to wake for a feed in the night depends very much on the individual baby. Some babies aged 6–8 weeks sleep through after the 10pm feed, while others won't do so until 10–12 weeks; some might take even longer. All babies will sleep through the night as soon as they are physically and mentally able, provided the daytime feeding and sleeping are being properly structured.

* Feeding in the night at the weaning stage will definitely affect the amount of solids a baby takes during the day, so getting the right amount of solids balanced with the correct amount of milk

is vital. Increasing solids too rapidly during the day can also cause problems as it can result in too small a milk feed at bedtime.

✿ Excessive amounts of fruit and vegetables in the late afternoon can cause the baby to poo in the middle of the night. Feeding your baby too much commercially prepared food often results in a low intake of protein, a further cause of night-time waking.

✿ During the early days of weaning it is advisable to keep a diary of what foods your baby eats and any reactions he has. The most common foods that I have found to cause night-time waking (if given to excess) in babies under six months are bananas, citrus fruits, tomatoes, sweet potatoes and carrots. I am not suggesting that you eliminate these from your baby's diet; simply keep a detailed food diary to help you spot any offending foods.

✿ With older babies and toddlers I am convinced that too much processed food high in sugar and additives can cause poor night-time sleep. Excessive amounts of sweets and chocolate certainly affect the behaviour and sleep of some toddlers, as do excessive amounts of fruit juice and squashes.

Daytime sleeping

It is absolutely vital that your child should have the right amount of sleep during the day, neither too much nor too little. Only then can you be sure of the good night's sleep that will naturally follow. Ideally, your baby's day should begin at 7am and end at 7pm, with daytime sleeps according to his age and needs. The amount and timing of naps is also important to avoid overtiredness.

Recommended day time sleep

Birth–4 weeks:	5 hours
4–8 weeks:	4–4$\frac{1}{2}$ hours
8–12 weeks:	3$\frac{1}{2}$ hours
3–6 months:	3 hours
6–12 months:	2$\frac{1}{2}$–3 hours
12–15 months:	2$\frac{1}{2}$ hours
18–24 months:	2 hours
2–2$\frac{1}{2}$ years:	1–2 hours
2$\frac{1}{2}$–3 years:	0–1 hour

✿ Allowing too much sleep during the day can result in difficulty in settling during the evening, or in middle-of-the-night wakings. But allowing too little can often result in worse problems. Many parents make the mistake of allowing their baby or toddler little or no sleep during the day in the belief that he will sleep better at night. In my experience, this rarely works, as the baby or toddler usually becomes so overtired and irritable that he is difficult to settle in the evening and is much more likely to wake up in the night.

✿ Striking the right balance takes planning and adjustment, but I think it is one of the best things you can do for your child. Aim to structure set times for your baby's daytime sleep and awake times, and encourage an awake period for babies under one month of 1–2 hours after daytime feeds. By one month, try to ensure that your baby is awake for a total of 6–8 hours between 7am and 7pm, and that he is awake for as much of a two-hour social time as possible. Keeping a diary of your baby's sleep patterns will help you to achieve this.

Morning naps

✿ A baby under one month of age is usually ready for a nap 1½–2 hours from the time he wakes up in the morning. By two months of age, most babies will manage to stay awake for two full hours.

✿ If the baby stays awake for longer than two hours, he will often become overtired and fight sleep. Overtiredness is one of the main causes of a baby not settling well at nap time, and care should be taken that this does not happen.

* By the time they reach six months, the majority of babies can stay awake for nearly two and a half hours.

* All babies should be woken no later than 10am if you want them to sleep for a longer time at 12 noon.

* At around one year of age most babies will cut right back on their morning nap, usually cutting it out altogether somewhere between 15 and 18 months.

Lunchtime naps

* A baby under one month is often ready for his nap around 11.30am, but by the time he reaches two months he can usually make it to 12 noon.

* Ideally, the lunchtime nap should be the longest of the day, as recent research shows that a nap between 12 noon and 2pm is deeper and more refreshing than a later nap because it co-incides with the baby's natural dip in alertness.

* Once a baby reaches six months of age and his morning nap becomes later, the lunchtime nap will also come later – usually around 12.30pm.

- Depending on how well the baby has slept at the morning nap, this nap usually lasts 2–2½ hours.

- At around one year of age this nap may cut back to one and a half hours if the baby is still having a full 45-minute nap in the morning, although it may lengthen again to two hours once the morning nap is dropped.

- The majority of babies will continue to need a nap at midday until they are two years of age, at which time they will gradually reduce the amount of time they sleep, cutting it out altogether somewhere between two and a half and three years of age.

Late-afternoon naps

- If a baby sleeps well at two earlier naps during the day, the late-afternoon nap should be the shortest of the three.

- A baby under eight weeks usually needs 30 minutes–1 hour. By the time they reach 12 weeks of age, the majority of babies who have slept well at lunchtime will need only a very short nap of 15–20 minutes in order to revive them enough for the bath and bedtime routine.

- As the late-afternoon nap is shorter than the earlier naps, it can be a good opportunity for you to try and get your baby used to sleeping in different environments such as a buggy or car-seat.

* The late-afternoon nap is usually dropped somewhere between three and six months of age.

* Allowing a baby to have a long sleep later in the day is often the reason he does not settle well at 7pm.

Bathtime and wind-down time

I think it is crucial to follow the same routine every night in order to allow your baby to establish the patterns that will lead him naturally towards a comfortable and refreshing sleep. Just like adults, babies appreciate the calming pleasures of a bath and a massage. It is also a wonderful time for you to bond with your baby: stay close so that he can see your face, and both of you can enjoy the soothing warm water and skin contact.

* You must allow enough time to settle your baby at sleep times. Make a note of how long he can stay awake before falling asleep, then make sure that you allow a 10- or 15-minute wind-down period before he goes to sleep.

* If he has just had a feed and is falling asleep on the breast or bottle, try to rouse him slightly before you put him down so that he is aware that he is going into his cot.

* Never attempt to bath a baby who is tired, hungry and getting near his feed time. Until he is near eight weeks, split the feed: give him half after he has had a short nap in the late afternoon, around 5pm; he can have the second half quietly in the nursery, just before he goes down into his cot. Wait a good 45 minutes after the 5pm feed before beginning the bath.

* Prepare everything in advance for the bath, making sure that you have laid out towels, nightclothes, creams and everything else needed.

* Close the curtains in the bedroom and lower the lighting. Make sure that the bedroom and bathroom are warm enough. Very young babies feel the cold more than adults, so you might have to put the heating on for a short spell on a cold day in the spring or summer.

* Keep the bedtime routine calm and quiet; once the bath is over, do not allow lots of visitors in the nursery as this can overstimulate the baby. With older babies and toddlers, talk quietly, using simple phrases. Do not get into long-winded conversations at this stage, and avoid games and activities that could cause them to become overexcited.

* Try to allow your baby 5–10 minutes to settle himself to sleep.

If he is getting very upset, pick him up and offer him more to eat. Resettle him in his cot again and leave him for a further 5–10 minutes. If he is still very unsettled, repeat the same procedure. You may find that for the first few nights you have to resettle him several times before he eventually falls asleep.

SOLUTIONS TO COMMON SLEEP PROBLEMS

Here (in alphabetical order) are the most common causes of sleep disturbance. As you will see, most of them are quite straightforward to deal with.

Colic

Excessive crying in babies under three months is more often than not diagnosed as colic. The colicky baby is usually described as being in great pain, screaming as he brings his knees up to his tummy, which is often distended and noisy. These long crying spells usually start in the late afternoon or early evening, and can last for several hours at a time. Experts are divided as to what causes colic, but the majority agree that there is no magical cure. Some take the view that colic normally disappears within three months and is something parents have to learn to live with. Sadly, for parents struggling to cope with a colicky baby, what should be the happiest time of their lives can turn out to be one of the most miserable, with no amount of feeding, rocking, cuddling and walking stopping the hard and excessive crying.

As many parents of a colicky baby can confirm, the colic does disappear at three months but, unfortunately, the sleeping problems do not. All the rocking and cuddling involved in trying to calm the baby can lead to the wrong sleep associations. He still refuses to settle in the evening and often wakes several times in the night. Each time he wakes he expects to be fed, rocked or cuddled back to sleep. This problem can continue for many months and often years.

I am frequently asked how I coped when my babies suffered from colic. The honest answer is that not one of the hundreds of babies I have helped care for has ever suffered from colic. I am convinced this is because I structured their feeding and sleeping from day one. My advice is always the same: follow a good routine that ensures the right feeding, sleeping and stimulation for your baby. If your baby is crying for hours every evening, it could be for one or more of the reasons described below. By eliminating all these possible causes and following the routine appropriate for your baby's age, you should find that his excessive crying is greatly reduced.

Tips for coping with colic

✿ Many breast-fed babies are very unsettled in the evening because their mother is tired and her milk supply is low. Try topping up your baby with a bottle of either expressed or formula milk after the evening feeds. If things improve, it will be clear that a low milk supply is the problem. I would advise that you try to increase your milk supply by expressing to ensure that a low milk supply does not become a long-term problem that could cause you to give up breast-feeding.

✿ If your baby is taking a top-up, but is crying a lot and difficult to settle in the evenings, it may be that he has got into the habit of being awake at this time. You could try taking the baby into your bed at 7pm and holding him in your arms (propped up with lots of pillows) until the 10pm feed. Sometimes a dummy is useful to get your baby off to sleep initially. When using this method I would suggest having the television on quietly so as not to get too bored! Usually I find that after only a couple of nights of this the baby has got into the habit of sleeping at this time and by the third night will go down swaddled and in his Moses basket beside your bed if you stay in the room with him. Then on the fourth or fifth night I would transfer the Moses basket back into the baby's room or put him back in his cot.

* Both breast-fed and bottle-fed babies should be fed no later than 2.15pm in the afternoon to ensure that they take a really good feed at 5–6.15pm.

* Babies fed on demand are more prone to colic. Gradually increase the times between feeds until your baby is feeding at the times recommended in my routines as appropriate for his age.

* Ensure that your baby is getting the right amount of daytime sleep.

* A baby who is screaming at every feed and arching his back midway through a feed could be suffering from reflux, a more serious medical condition than colic. In this case, seek medical advice.

Difficulties in settling

* A baby who is allowed to fall asleep on the breast or bottle and is then put in the cot will be more likely to have disruptive nap times. When he comes to a light sleep 20–45 minutes after falling asleep, he will be less likely to settle himself back to sleep without your help. If your baby falls asleep while feeding, put him on the changing mat and rearrange his nappy. This should rouse him enough to go down in the cot semi-awake.

* Overtiredness is the major cause of babies not settling and not sleeping well during the day. A baby under three months who is

allowed to stay awake longer than two hours at a time may become so overtired that he goes on to fight sleep for a further two hours.

* A close eye should be kept on all babies after they have been awake for one and a half hours so that you do not miss the cue for sleep.

* Overhandling prior to sleep time is another major problem with young babies. Everybody wants just one little cuddle. Unfortunately, several little cuddles add up and can leave the baby fretful, overtired and difficult to settle. Your baby is not a toy. Do not feel guilty about restricting the handling in the early weeks, especially prior to sleep time. Allow a wind-down time of at least 20 minutes before naps, avoiding games and activities.

* With all babies, regardless of age, avoid excessive talking at put-down time. Talk quietly and calmingly, repeating the same phrases.

* The wrong sleep associations can also cause long-term sleep problems. It is essential that a baby goes down in his cot awake and learns to settle himself. For a baby who has already learnt the wrong sleep associations, this problem can rarely be solved without some amount of crying. Fortunately, the majority of babies will learn to settle themselves within a few days.

Early morning waking

I believe that how parents deal with early morning waking during the first few months will help determine whether their baby will become a child who is an early riser. Hunger should always be looked at as the first cause of a baby waking too early, and once you are sure that it is not the problem, look carefully at daytime sleep habits (your sleep diary will help here). Other possible causes of early waking include nappy rash and teething (see pages 31 and 33).

✿ With babies under two months, too small a feed in the middle of the night (between 1am and 5am) is often a cause of early waking. The middle-of-the-night feed should never be reduced until the baby has shown that he can sleep happily to 7am for at least one week. Then it can gradually be reduced every few nights by a small amount provided he is sleeping through to 7am and continues to gain weight.

✿ With babies between two and four months who are sleeping through most of the night, too small a feed at 10pm is often the cause of early waking, so they should be offered a top-up of expressed or formula milk from a bottle if they are emptying both breasts.

- During the first few weeks, a baby who is feeding at 2–2.30am may wake around 6am and genuinely need to feed. However, it is essential to treat this feed like a night-time feed. It should be done as quickly and quietly as possible, in the glow of just a small night-light and without talking or eye contact. The baby should then be settled back to sleep until 7–7.30am. If possible, avoid changing the nappy as this usually wakes the baby too much.

- During the first 2–3 months it is important to have the baby fully awake at the 10pm feed for at least an hour. Once the baby is sleeping through regularly to 7am for at least a week, you can gradually cut back on the time he is awake at 10pm. Reducing it by 10 minutes every three nights, provided he continues to sleep through to 7am, will ensure that he does not end up waking earlier.

- Once the baby is over four months old, is taking only a small feed at 10pm, is awake for only 20 minutes and solids are well established, this waking time can be dropped. Once the 10pm feed has been dropped, it is important to encourage your baby to stay awake until 7pm.

- When the baby is over four months, parents often drop the 10pm feed before he is taking enough solids. Ensure that your baby is well established on solids for at least two weeks and taking only a very small feed before dropping the 10pm feed. Once he drops it, he may also start to wake up early because he is not getting enough to eat at the 7pm feed. If so, offer him a top-up after this feed.

✿ Between six and 12 months nearly all babies are well established on three solid meals a day and three milk feeds. Provided a baby is receiving the right balance of protein, carbohydrates, vegetables and fruit, plus three full milk feeds a day, he should not be waking up because he is hungry.

✿ Between six and nine months many babies who have slept regularly to 7am will often start to wake up earlier in the morning if you have not pushed the morning and lunchtime nap on to 9.30am and 12.30pm. If your baby is starting to wake up earlier and earlier, try gradually moving his first nap of the day forward by five minutes every three or four days so that he will eventually be happy to go down later for his middle-of-the-day nap.

✿ If your baby is waking early and sleeping 1–2 hours in the morning and only one hour in the afternoon, gradually cut back on his morning nap by 10 minutes every 3–4 days, until he is sleeping no more than 30–40 minutes. This should have the knock-on effect of him sleeping longer in the afternoon and prevent overtiredness keeping him awake later. If he will sleep for only an hour or less at the second nap, try offering him a small drink of milk, water or well-diluted juice before he goes down in case thirst is preventing him from sleeping longer at this time.

✿ Avoid using a night-light or leaving the door open.

✿ All babies under six months sleep better if tucked in securely. Babies who work their way up the cot and get out of the covers will benefit from being put in a lightweight, 0.5 tog 100 per cent cotton sleeping bag and being tucked in with a sheet.

✿ Once a baby starts to move around the cot and is capable of rolling, I would advise that you remove the sheets and blankets and use only a sleeping bag suitable for the time of year to prevent coldness waking him up.

Nappy rash

✿ If your baby or toddler's bottom becomes affected with nappy rash, it can be very uncomfortable and disrupt sleep. You will need to change his nappies even more frequently than usual. Use an unperfumed baby oil and cotton wool to clean the sensitive area – it will be less painful than using water or baby wipes.

✿ A rash that persists after a few days should be seen by a doctor as it may be a candida rash, often referred to as thrush, which will need a special anti-fungal cream.

✿ Check and change your baby or toddler's nappy every couple of hours regardless of whether he has had a bowel movement.

✿ If you use a barrier cream, apply only a thin layer. Too much will reduce the absorbency of disposable nappies. Never use baby powder as it can clog the baby's skin, and even the tiniest amount can prove fatal if it reaches his lungs.

✿ Remove your baby or toddler's nappy and expose his bottom to fresh air at least twice a day.

Rolling over

✿ Between the ages of six and nine months the majority of babies start to roll from their back to their front, and until they learn to roll back again they can get quite upset. You may find that for a few weeks you have to help your baby settle back to sleep by rolling him back.

✿ Help your baby practise rolling during his playtime. Once he has become confident about rolling back and forth from his tummy to his back, it is advisable not to rush to him the minute he cries out. Allow him a short spell to settle himself, otherwise he will become dependent on you to help him get back to sleep.

Standing up

✿ Between nine and 12 months some babies will start pulling themselves up in the cot, but will not be able to get themselves back down to the sleeping position. Again, they will need some help getting back down until they have learnt to do it themselves.

✿ It is a good idea when settling the baby at sleep time to put him in the cot standing and, holding his hands, teach him how to hold on to the bars and lower himself down to whatever sleeping position he prefers.

Teething

✿ If you are convinced that your baby's night-time wakings are caused by severe teething pain, I suggest you seek advice from your doctor regarding the use of paracetamol. While genuine teething pain can cause a few disrupted nights, it should never last for several weeks.

✿ If your baby is teething and waking in the night but quickly settles back to sleep when given a cuddle or a dummy, teething is probably not the real cause of the waking. A baby who is genuinely bothered by teething pain would be difficult to settle back to sleep. He would also show signs of discomfort during the day, not just at night.

Wind

The method of feeding can make a difference to the amount of wind a baby suffers from, so look at the appropriate tips below.

Tips for windy breast-fed babies

✿ These babies do not normally take in as much air as those who are bottle-fed, and may not bring up wind after each feed. If your baby has not brought up his wind within a few minutes and seems happy, it is best not to spend ages trying to get the wind up, as the endless rubbing and patting on the back can actually cause more upset than the wind itself. A baby who is genuinely bothered by wind will scream and scream after a feed – nothing will console him until he manages to burp.

✿ Make sure that the baby is correctly positioned on the breast. It is worth arranging a home visit from your health visitor or your NCT breast-feeding counsellor, who will teach you how to position your baby on the breast correctly.

✿ A breast-fed baby's wind can be caused by something the mother is eating. The pain usually occurs 12–16 hours after she has eaten the offending food. The main foods I have found to cause a reaction in babies, if eaten in excess by the mother, are dairy products, citrus foods, mushrooms and tomatoes. While tea, coffee, sugar and chocolate do not appear to cause wind, I do find that if taken in excess, they can cause irritability in some babies. If you suspect a certain food may be causing your baby's wind, try cutting out that particular food for several days. If there is a marked improvement, wait a further week before introducing the food again, and, even then, do so gradually. However, if you find that the smallest amount of the suspect food causes your baby excessive wind, I would advise you to discuss this with your health visitor or doctor.

✿ It is essential that a breast-feeding mother eats a varied and healthy diet and consumes an extra 500 calories a day. Try to avoid eating too many convenience foods that are loaded with additives and empty starches. Also remember that this is not the time for dieting or excessive exercise; losing weight too quickly will not only reduce the amount of milk you produce, but could also result in the toxins that are accumulated in the fatty tissue being released into your breast milk. Some experts believe that these toxins can cause irritability in some babies.

Tips for windy bottle-fed babies

✿ While babies who are bottle-fed tend to take in more wind than breast-fed babies, this should not create a problem as long as the baby is given the opportunity to burp once during the feed and once at the end. If your bottle-fed baby has problems bringing up his wind and suffers a lot of discomfort as a result, check the amount of formula he is taking and how often he is feeding. A formula-fed baby needs 75–90ml (2½–3oz) of formula per pound of his body weight each day. I believe that overfeeding is one of the major causes of excessive wind. Occasionally, a very hungry baby may need a little more milk a day, but if your baby is drinking 150ml (5oz) or more in excess of the recommended daily amount, he could be overfeeding, and this can cause severe wind pains.

✿ Look at the type of bottle you are using. I have found that the wide-necked bottle by Avent, with its specially designed teat, helps reduce the amount of air that a baby takes in.

✿ Pay extra attention when making up the formula feed: follow the manufacturer's instructions to the letter and make sure that you shake the bottle well, then shake it again to ensure that the water and formula are thoroughly mixed together.

✿ Before feeding your baby, loosen and rescrew the ring and teat back on to the bottle to release any excess air.

✿ Ensure that you keep the bottle tilted so that the teat is filled with milk at all times. Keeping the baby in a more upright position during and after feeding also helps reduce the amount of air he takes in.

✿ Laying the baby flat on his back for a couple of minutes, then slowly raising him to a sitting position may help to release trapped air. Alternatively, lay the baby flat on his tummy with his head to one side while gently rubbing his back.

✿ Some parents find that colic drops, such as Infacol, help their baby's excessive or trapped wind. There are also natural alternatives, such as Chamomilla drops or Windypops, which contain chamomile, fennel, catnip and lemon balm. Whether using conventional or alternative treatments, it is always advisable to discuss the correct dosages with a health visitor or qualified homoeopath.

TWINS

The idea of having all the normal sleeping problems multiplied by two can sometimes seem overwhelming – but don't panic. The crucial thing is to establish a routine. It is hard work with twins, but it is achievable. I know because I've done it, and so can you. Although it normally takes longer to get twins sleeping through the night, nearly all the sets I have cared for were sleeping through the night from their last feed at 10–11pm to 6–7am in the morning by 12–14 weeks.

Tips for avoiding long-term sleep problems with twins

✿ Do not allow your babies to go longer than three hours between feeds (from the beginning of one feed to the beginning of the next) until they reach a weight of at least 3kg (7lb). It is of no benefit to let them sleep longer between feeds as their tummies are so small that they need to feed little and often to gain as much weight as possible in the early days. Once they have reached 3kg (7lb), their tummies will be able to hold more milk at a feed, and then it is possible to let them go slightly longer.

✿ In the early days you might find things easier if you can keep the babies on one level for most of the day. Trying to get them up and down stairs between feeds, particularly in the morning, can be very exhausting. I have found that having the steriliser, all the equipment and a small fridge upstairs is a lifesaver in the very early days.

* Take turns on night duty. If possible, try to fit a small futon or single bed into the nursery to allow the off-duty parent to get a good night's sleep in their own bedroom. Planning the nights so that each parent gets a stretch of sleep is very important. I used to get the mother to go to bed at 9pm and the father to do the feeds between 10pm and midnight. By the time the first twin woke in the night, normally around 1 or 2am, the mother had had at least three or four hours' sleep.

* Twins normally need more sleep during the first month than single babies, but they also need more feeds. Sometimes only an hour can elapse between feeding one twin and the other one waking up. It is very important to accept whatever help you can get in the early days. Do not feel guilty about asking relatives and friends to help with shopping or household chores so that you can catch up on extra sleep during the day.

* Settle the twins in separate cots from the very beginning. I have found that they are much more likely to disturb each other when they are put to sleep in the same cot.

✿ I usually found that one twin would start to fight sleep at around three weeks of age. I would then put him in a separate room for several days so that the other twin wouldn't be woken. However, I always had to go through a stage where they had to get used to each other's crying. This could be very difficult because just as one got off to sleep, the other one would start up. As long as I knew they were well fed and ready to sleep, I did not interfere with this settling process. I had learnt from experience that twins who were never allowed to get used to each other's crying would often continue to be difficult to settle in the evening and would go on waking up several times a night for most of their first year, and perhaps even longer.

SLEEP PROBLEMS IN OLDER BABIES AND TODDLERS

After the difficult and stressful early days of establishing sleeping patterns for your baby, you might look forward to trouble-free nights for ever more. Nothing is that simple, of course. As your child grows up, new problems can arise. However, there are simple solutions to most of these challenges.

Bedtime difficulties

This term applies to a child who has previously settled easily at bedtime but now starts resisting sleep and refusing to fall asleep alone, protesting loudly when his parents leave the room. He could develop night-time fears and anxieties. Fear of the dark and talk of monsters are very common at this stage, and should be dealt with sensitively but firmly. In my experience, a child who has previously settled well but suddenly becomes dependent on either of his parents being in the room while he falls asleep will very quickly learn the wrong sleep associations. He will more than likely start to wake up in the night and expect one of his parents to be there until he goes back to sleep.

* Watch out for the child beginning to use delaying tactics at bedtime, asking for yet another story or drink, or to use the potty. This is the first sign of a problem.

* If your child is in a cot, use the checking method: settle your child and leave him alone in the cot, then check him every 5–10 minutes gradually increasing the time between checks each night, without engaging in conversation or touching him, until he has gone to sleep. This way he will not feel that you are totally abandoning him and will also realise that you are not going to keep giving in to his constant demands.

* If your child has already moved to a bed, you will probably find that he will keep getting out of bed if left alone, so use the gradual withdrawal method: spend 10 minutes in the room, then leave for two minutes, explaining that you will be back in a minute. Repeat, gradually increasing the time you are out of the room, until the child is asleep.

* If the child asks for the light to be left on, I would leave a socket night-light on until the child goes to sleep on the understanding that he lies quietly in bed.

* Between two and three years the majority of children will have cut down dramatically on their daytime sleep, and by the time they reach three years of age, most will have given up the daytime nap altogether. If your child is becoming more difficult to settle at night, it is important to make sure that he is not having too much sleep during the day.

Comforter dependency

Between six and nine months nearly all babies begin to develop an attachment to a comforter. Some become dependent on a blanket or muslin cloth; others may choose a soft toy or use their thumb or a dummy. The majority of experts agree that the use of a comforter is a normal part of a baby's development, but most stress the importance of a child not becoming over-dependent on it because, for one thing, it is a disaster if it gets lost. By three years of age most children become less reliant on their comforter, and by the time they reach five years they have usually abandoned it altogether.

* When you notice your baby or toddler becoming attached to a certain object, limit its use to bedtime or special rest time in the house. Do not allow him to drag it from room to room or on trips out, though obviously you will need to take it on holidays and overnight visits. Otherwise, be insistent that the blanket, cloth or toy stays in the cot.

* If possible, try to purchase a duplicate, as this will allow for frequent washing and provide you with a replacement if the comforter becomes damaged or lost.

* If you find that your young baby or toddler is getting more and more dependent on a comforter, is withdrawn and not interacting in the way he used to, there could be other underlying emotional reasons. Talk to your GP or health visitor about any concerns you may have.

Moving to a big bed

In my experience, transferring a toddler to a big bed before he is ready can be a major cause of night-time waking. Many parents make this transfer between 18 months and two years of age, often prompted by the fact that a new baby is on the way and the cot will be needed. Other parents listen to the advice of friends who say that their toddler sleeps much better now that he is in a bed. To me this implies that their toddler's sleeping habits were probably not very good in the first place!

The majority of my clients leave their toddlers in a cot until they are nearly three years of age. And because all these toddlers are still in a sleeping bag, the possibility of them trying to climb out of the cot never arises. If a cot is needed for a second baby, many parents choose to buy a second cot, or a cot bed into which the toddler can be transferred before the new baby arrives. This can eventually be used as a first bed for the toddler.

Big bed considerations

✿ A toddler who is transferred to a bed too early is more likely to wake up early or get up in the night. He is inclined to get more upset than an older child when parents try to settle him back to sleep in his own bed, and often ends up sleeping in his parents' bed.

✿ The arrival of a new baby often prompts the toddler to get out of bed if he hears the baby crying in the night. He quickly learns to demand the same night-time attention as the baby – feeds and a cuddle.

✿ A toddler who is being potty trained and sleeping in a bed will be more likely to take his nappy off in the night, even if he is not able to get through the night without a nappy.

✿ Once the nappy is abandoned at night, a potty and night-light usually have to be put in the toddler's room. In my experience, toddlers under three years of age who are sleeping in a bed and who need to have a night-light are much more likely to wake in the night and be difficult to settle back to sleep.

New baby

Acquiring a new brother or sister can often lead toddlers who have previously slept well to start waking up in the night. The best way to deal with this is to go straight to your toddler and reassure him that you are there. Try to keep the reassurance brief and do not get involved in conversation or resort to taking him out of his bed.

In my experience, toddlers who are still sleeping in a cot seem to have less waking in the night than those who have been transferred to a bed just prior to the birth of the baby. Within a few weeks, most toddlers settle down to sleeping well at night again. If not, try some of the following ideas.

Tips for dealing with toddlers after a baby arrives

* Establish regular daytime naps when your baby is put to sleep away from the toddler so that you can give the older child your undivided attention at regular times during the day. This will help him feel more secure than a toddler who is suddenly faced with having to share his mother every waking hour of the day.

* If your toddler doesn't seem overly interested in the baby, try not to force the issue. He will start to take an interest in his own time; pressuring him to do so before he is ready will only make him feel more resentful towards the baby.

* In the very early days try to structure as many of the baby's feeds as possible for when your toddler is not around – for example, before he gets up in the morning and around 2pm when he is having his nap. Of course there will be times when he is around when the baby is feeding, but until he gets used to sharing you with the baby, the less he sees the baby on your breast the better.

Nightmares

Nightmares are most common between the ages of three and six years, but I believe that they can start much earlier. I've often had to deal with children as young as two years old who were experiencing nightmares. If your child has always slept well and suddenly wakes up screaming during the second half of the night, he is probably having a bad dream and should be comforted and reassured immediately. Since a child of this age is still not able to grasp the difference between dreaming and reality, it is pointless trying to convince him that the monster doesn't exist. I have found the best approach is to follow the advice of Dr John Pearce and Dr Miriam Stoppard, and work out a plan for how best to deal with the monster, such as making the monster fall into a hole, or saying a magic spell to make it disappear.

Tips for dealing with nightmares

* If your child is repeatedly waking up crying over several weeks, look at what is happening during the day. Keep a detailed diary of his daytime activities and details of the nightmare – this will often help to pinpoint something or someone that could be causing him distress.

- Bedtime stories and videos that involve violence or have a frightening storyline can cause some children to have nightmares, so they should be monitored to ensure that they are suitable for your child's age.

- If you have an older child, it might be necessary to stagger the bedtimes for a short while so that the younger one is not subjected to anything frightening. Even a story such as *Little Red Riding Hood* is enough to trigger nightmares in a child under three years.

- Sometimes it is possible to pin down nightmares to a certain activity. For example, your child may feel threatened by an aggressive child at playgroup, or have developed a fear of certain animals, or particular people, such as policemen.

- A fear of the dark often contributes to a child having more frequent nightmares. Installing a low-voltage night-light and buying a special new toy that will chase the monsters away often helps.

- Frequent late bedtimes, which usually result in a child getting overtired and irritable, are often a cause of nightmares, particularly when parents get short-tempered and cross. The child ends up going to bed exhausted, fretful and feeling unloved. He may then wake in the night, remember how cross his parents were, and get upset and cry out. Although he will blame a bad dream, often the real cause of crying out is a need for reassurance that his parents are no longer angry with him.

Night terrors

As they are very different from nightmares, night terrors need to be dealt with differently. A child experiencing a night terror will usually wake up screaming during the earlier part of the night, usually within 1–4 hours of falling asleep. Terrors occur during the deep sleep known as non-REM (rapid eye movement) sleep, and although a child having a night terror will scream, thrash around and have his eyes open, he is rarely awake. Whereas a child having a nightmare can be comforted, it can be very difficult to calm and comfort a child having a night terror. It is very distressing for parents to watch a child having a night terror because he appears to be terrified, often sweating profusely and screaming as if he is experiencing something horrific.

In my experience, night terrors are much more common among children who become overtired because they have inconsistent daytime and bedtime routines.

Tips for dealing with night terrors

✿ A night terror usually lasts between 10 and 20 minutes, and provided the child is not woken up, he will quickly settle back to sleep once the terror is over.

✿ The majority of experts advise parents not to hold the child unless he shows signs of wanting to be held, as it often makes matters worse if he becomes fully awake and is unaware of what has been happening. It is better just to stay close by so that, if needed, you can prevent him from injuring himself.

✿ It is important not to mention the terror the following day, as your child may get very upset if questioned about something of which he has no recollection.

Night-time feeding

If your toddler is still needing to be fed to sleep and wakes several times a night, refusing to settle back to sleep without a feed, it is important that you look very closely at his daytime feeding before you embark on any further sleep remedies. They will not work if the toddler is hungry. In my experience, night-time hunger is a result of demand-feeding in the very early days: the milk feeds were not structured properly, so the baby was never given the opportunity to increase his daytime feeding. A vicious cycle soon evolves of the baby needing to make up his daily nutritional needs during the night because he did not feed well in the day, along with the wrong association of falling asleep on the breast or bottle, which leads to a very serious problem.

As night-time feeding is more than an association problem, it is important that steps are taken to improve the daytime feeding. (See the next chapter for more information about feeding.)

Overtiredness

Not getting enough sleep during the day can cause problems at bedtime, particularly with a child under 30 months who has dropped his daytime sleep. During this stage, daytime activities have usually increased, demanding more of the child's mental and physical energy. Even the most easygoing of children can start to play up at bedtime, and overtiredness is one of the main reasons why a child who used to settle easily at bedtime becomes more difficult.

✿ A child who used to settle happily at around 7.30pm may need the bedtime routine brought forward so that he is in bed by 7pm, particularly if he has not had a nap that day.

IF MORE HELP IS NEEDED . . .

This chapter addresses the most common sleep problems, but if you still find yourself suffering with a child who is either too entrenched in bad sleep habits or who doesn't respond to the routines above, there *is* more you can do. A small number of parents may need to embark on a more complex programme of sleep training in order to help their babies learn to sleep comfortably and easily. This is all explained simply and clearly in *The Complete Sleep Guide for Contented Babies and Toddlers*, where I go into problems and solutions in greater depth, and where I include case studies that might match the kind of problems you are having.

2
Milk Feeding

I stand wholeheartedly behind the theory that breast is best. It's the most natural way to feed your baby, provides him with all the nutrition he needs, has benefits for both mother and child, and it comes completely free. I'm not alone in supporting breast-feeding. Immediately after the baby's birth, midwives encourage mothers to put the baby to the breast and guide them through the techniques of positioning and latching the baby on. There are also lots of organisations dedicated to promoting breast-feeding, counsellors to help new mothers in the early weeks, and many books written on the subject. Perhaps it's surprising, therefore, that, according to various surveys, 33 per cent of breast-feeding mothers give up before the baby is one month old. It just goes to show that what is natural is not always easy.

Mothers' reasons for stopping breast-feeding

✿ They feel they are not producing enough milk.

✿ Cracked nipples and pain.

✿ The baby is discontented and not thriving.

✿ Exhaustion owing to the baby feeding for hours at a time, often throughout the whole night.

✿ They don't enjoy it and start to dread feeding times.

I think this is very sad – not least because there are solutions to the first four problems. But if a mother really feels she cannot go on breast-feeding, then she certainly shouldn't be pressurised into continuing. Hundreds of thousands of babies throughout the world do wonderfully well, physically and emotionally, on formula milk, and the most important thing is that you and your baby are happy. If breast-feeding is not for you, establish bottle-feeding and enjoy your baby. There are plenty of discontented people in the world who were breast-fed – it's not a magic answer for a happy child.

Whether a baby is breast-fed or bottle-fed, it will still take time and perseverance to establish a routine. I've established my feeding routines over many years and, in my experience, they seem the best way to answer a baby's needs: within two weeks there is a feeding pattern (which will naturally help a sleep pattern), and the baby is happy and gaining weight.

SUCCESSFUL BREAST-FEEDING

For many reasons that I won't go into here, I have found that demand-feeding – a very woolly and misleading term, I think – is not the best way to feed a baby. Instead, I advise beginning with little and often in the early days in order to stimulate the breast to produce enough milk, moving towards a set routine as your milk comes in between the third and fifth day and the baby begins to need longer, more satisfying feeds.

Tips for comfortable breast-feeding

✿ Prepare what you need for a feed in advance: a comfortable chair with arms and a straight back, and perhaps a footstool; a drink of water; some soothing music.

✿ Make sure you are sitting comfortably with your back straight.

- The baby should be well supported and in the correct position – his tummy to your tummy – and his mouth should be open wide enough for him to take all the nipple and as much of the areola as he can manage into his mouth. Take time to make sure of these things before you start.

- When your milk comes in it might be difficult to latch the baby on to the breast: expressing a little milk before feeding may help.

- Chilled flannels placed on the breasts can reduce the discomfort of engorgement.

- Some mothers find that tucking chilled cabbage leaves into their bra between feeds can provide relief for sore breasts.

- Rest as much as possible between feeds.

- Do not go too long between meals, and do eat small, healthy snacks in between.

- Drink plenty of water.

- Never allow your baby to suck on an empty breast – this will lead to very painful nipples.

Feeding from birth

The routines which can be found in *The New Contented Little Baby Book* provide several benefits: they establish a good milk supply;

help avoid cracked nipples and painful engorgement; help you to learn your baby's different needs; satisfy the baby and prevent the feeding-all-night syndrome; help keep you relaxed and comfortable.

* Start by offering the baby five minutes on each breast every three hours between 6am and midnight, increasing the time by a few minutes each day until the milk comes in.

* **Remember that the three-hour stretch between feeds is timed from the beginning of one feed to the beginning of the next**, so a baby starting to feed at 7am would need to start his next feed at 10am.

* By the time the milk arrives, the sucking time on the breast should be about 15–20 minutes.

* Many babies will get enough milk from the first breast to last three hours before needing another feed.

* If your baby has totally emptied the first breast, burp him and change his nappy. Offer the second breast – if he needs more, he will take it. If not, start him off on that breast at the next feed. You could leave a small piece of tissue or cotton wool inside the cup of your nursing bra to remind you which breast to feed from next.

* If your baby is demanding food long before three hours have passed, he should be offered both breasts at each feed.

* It is essential that he empties the first breast before moving on to the second. Breast milk is made up of fore milk and hind milk. It might take the baby 20–25 minutes to reach the hind milk, which is three times fattier than the fore milk and therefore better for satisfying hunger.

* You can tell when the baby reaches the hind milk as his sucking will slow down and he will pause for longer between sucks.

* If your baby is feeding from both breasts at each feed, start the next feed on the last breast he fed from so that each one is totally emptied every second feed.

* Gently squeezing your nipple between thumb and forefinger lets you know if there is any milk still in the breast.

Expressing milk

This can be of enormous help in combining breast-feeding with a routine – in fact, I'd go so far as to say it's essential if you'd like to keep your baby in an established feeding routine. The simple reason for this is that the breast produces milk on a supply and demand basis. In the early days very few babies will empty both breasts; by the end of the second week, milk production balances out and most mothers will produce exactly the amount the baby needs. But you will run into trouble when the baby goes through a growth spurt, as happens in the third and fourth week, and suddenly demands more milk. Without expressing, you will probably have to go back to three-hourly feeds and night feeding. This has knock-on effects with sleeping and can disrupt all the hard work you've put into establishing a routine.

Mothers who express in the early days will always be producing more milk than their baby needs. When the baby goes through a growth spurt, his increased appetite can be satisfied simply by expressing less milk at the early morning feeds. Expressing will also help avoid the problems of a low milk supply.

Tips for expressing milk successfully

✿ The best time to express is in the morning when the breasts are fuller. It will usually be easier if done at the beginning of a feed and will give the breast slightly longer to make more milk for the next feed.

✿ Either express one breast just prior to feeding your baby, or feed your baby from one breast, then express from the second breast before offering him the remainder of his feed.

✿ Some mothers find it easier to express while they are feeding the baby on the other breast.

- In the early days you will need to allow at least 15 minutes to express 60–90ml (2–3oz) milk at the morning feeds, and up to 30 minutes at the evening expressing times. The more you practise, the easier it will become.

- Try to keep expressing times quiet and relaxed. Some mothers find it helpful to keep a photo of their baby close by, while others like to watch television or chat to their partners. See what works best for you.

- An electric, heavy-duty pump, like the kind used in hospitals, is the best way to express milk in the early days as the suction is designed to imitate a baby's rhythm. They are expensive to buy, but can be hired more cheaply. It is worth investing in an attachment that enables both breasts to be expressed at once to save time when you express at the 10pm feed.

- Once you are confident and well practised at expressing, and your milk supply is good, it is possible to use a hand pump or a commercial electric pump with good results.

- A relaxing warm bath or shower will encourage milk to flow more easily. Also gently massaging the breasts before and during expressing will help.

- Store expressed milk by freezing it. Specially designed bags are available from baby shops.

If you would like to increase your milk supply, there is a detailed plan for doing so in *The New Contented Little Baby Book*.

BOTTLE-FEEDING

A bottle-fed baby will need as much guidance into a routine as a breast-fed one. The main difference in feeding a baby formula (apart from the fact that someone else can give feeds) is that you don't have to worry about what you eat and drink. If you have decided to bottle-feed, the same routines as breast-feeding should be followed. Your baby may be happier to go longer than three hours after the 7am feed. If you need to split feeds, such as before and after a bath, use two smaller, separate feeds.

Health authorities advise that a baby under four months needs 75ml (2½oz) of milk for each pound of his body weight; a baby weighing around 3kg (7lb) would need approximately 510ml (18oz) a day. That amount would be divided into six feeds a day. This is only a guideline; hungrier babies might need an extra 30ml (1oz) at some feeds. If your baby is one of these, try to ensure that you structure the feeds so that he is taking the bigger ones at the right time, i.e. 7am, 10.30am or 10.30pm. If you allow him to get into the habit of having bigger feeds in the middle of the night, it will eventually have the knock-on effect of his not being so hungry will he wakes in the morning. A vicious circle emerges, where he needs to feed in the night because he does not feed enough during the day.

The same guidelines apply as for breast-feeding. Aim to get the baby to take most of his daily milk requirements between 7am and 11pm. This way he will need only a small feed in the middle of the night, and will eventually drop it altogether.

Note that there are two main brands of formula milk: both are approved by the health authorities and there is very little difference between them.

Tips for successful bottle-feeding

❖ Never heat up formula in the microwave: either use an electric bottle warmer or stand the bottle in a jug of boiling water.

❖ Always test the temperature of a feed before giving it to your baby. Just shake a few drops onto the inside of your wrist; it should feel lukewarm.

❖ Never reheat milk that has already been heated; this increases bacteria levels and can lead to upset tummies.

❖ You will soon get into the routine of making up the feeds needed for the next 24 hours. Choose a quiet time and carefully follow the manufacturer's instructions. Discard any leftover feed from the previous day and do not save unfinished feeds.

- Use a feed that has been heated up within one hour.

- Have an extra bottle of boiled water in the fridge for making up emergency feeds.

- You must pay the utmost attention to hygiene: sterilise all the feeding equipment and ensure that preparation and storage areas are spotlessly clean. A handy tip is to keep a separate kettle for boiling water for feeds – then you can be sure fresh water is used each time and only boiled once.

- As with breast-feeding, prepare everything in advance and ensure that you are sitting comfortably.

- Bottle-feeding can lead to the baby taking in more air than during breast-feeding; some babies will take most of their feed, burp and then want a break of 10–15 minutes before finishing the remainder. Allow up to 40 minutes for a full feed.

- If you find your baby is taking a very long time to feed, or keeps falling asleep halfway through, it could be because the hole in the teat is too small; move on to a medium-flow teat.

- It is easy for bottle-fed babies to gain weight too quickly if they are allowed feeds well in excess of the recommended amounts. A few extra ounces a day should not create a problem, but overeating babies will soon not be satisfied by milk alone.

BURPING

It is important to follow your baby's lead regarding when to stop and wind him. If you constantly interrupt his feed to try and get his wind up, he will probably become so upset and frustrated that the crying will cause more wind than the feed itself. Very few babies need to be burped more than once during a feed and once at the end.

* A breast-feeding baby will pull himself off the breast when he is ready to burp. If he has not done so by the end of the first breast, you can try burping him before putting him on the second breast.

* Bottle-fed babies will normally drink half to three-quarters of their feed, then pull themselves off to be burped.

* Regardless of whether you are breast-feeding or bottle-feeding, if the baby is in the correct position, he should bring his wind up quickly and easily both during and at the end of the feed. If your baby does not bring up the wind within a few minutes, it is best to leave it and try later. More often than not he will bring it up after he has been laid flat for his nappy change.

* Occasionally a baby passing excessive wind from his bottom can suffer considerable discomfort and become very distressed. A breast-feeding mother should keep a close eye on her diet to

see if something particular is causing the wind. Citrus fruits and drinks taken in excess can sometimes cause severe wind in babies. The other culprits are chocolate and excessive intake of dairy foods.

✿ Special care should be taken to make sure that a breast-fed baby is reaching the hind milk. Too much fore milk can cause explosive bowel movements and excessive passing of wind.

✿ With a bottle-fed baby who is already feeding from special anti-colic bottles, the cause of excessive wind is usually overfeeding. If your baby is regularly drinking 90–180ml (3–6oz) a day more than the amount advised on the packet, and is consistently putting on more than 250g (8oz) of weight each week, cut back on a couple of his feeds (either the 2.30pm or the 5pm) for a few days to see if there is any improvement. A 'sucky' baby could be offered a dummy after the smaller feeds to satisfy his sucking needs.

DIFFICULT FEEDERS

There are some babies who fuss and fret within minutes of being put on the breast or being offered the bottle; I've often found this with babies who've undergone a difficult birth. If you find that your baby becomes tense and fretful during feeds, try to avoid having visitors at such times. No matter how well-meaning family and friends may be, it is impossible to keep things completely calm and quiet if you are having to make conversation.

Tips for feeding tense or fretful babies

* Avoid overstimulation and handing the baby from person to person, especially before a feed.

* Give the feed in a quiet room with a calm atmosphere. Apart from perhaps one person to offer practical help and emotional support, no other person should be allowed in the room.

* Prepare everything needed for the feed well in advance.

* Try to make sure that you have rested and eaten.

* Turn off the television and unplug the telephone during a feed.

* Play some calm music while feeding.

* When the baby wakes for his feed, do not change his nappy as this might trigger off crying. It is very important to prevent the baby becoming tense before a feed.

* Try swaddling him firmly in a soft cotton sheet to prevent him thrashing his arms and legs around.

* Make sure that you are comfortable before you start feeding.

* Do not attempt to latch the baby on to the breast or put the bottle

straight in his mouth if he is crying. Hold him firmly in the feeding position and calm him down with continuous gentle patting on the back.

✿ Try holding a dummy in his mouth. Once he has calmed down and has sucked steadily for a few minutes, very quickly ease the dummy out and offer him the breast or the bottle.

When happy babies won't feed . . .

If your baby has been feeding well and suddenly starts to refuse the breast or bottle, it could be because he is feeling unwell. Ear infections can easily go undetected and are a very common cause of a baby not wanting to feed. If your baby shows any of the following signs, it would be advisable to consult your doctor:

✿ sudden loss of appetite, and becoming upset when offered a feed.

✿ disruption to the normal sleep pattern.

✿ suddenly becoming clingy or whingey.

✿ becoming lethargic and unsociable.

FEEDING TWINS

The guidelines given for feeding a single baby also apply to twins, but there are some ways to make dealing with two hungry babies at the same time easier.

✿ In my experience, staggering the feeds by 20 minutes means that you will, in the long term, not end up with two babies screaming for food at the same time. This is very important once the mother is left on her own to look after both babies. Waking one baby at 6.45am and offering most of the feed means that he should then be happy to sit in his chair for a short spell while you wake and give the second baby most of his feed. Once the second baby has had most of his feed, he should be happy to sit in his chair while you change the first baby's nappy and offer him the remainder of the feed. You can then go back to the second baby and change his nappy before offering him the remainder of his feed.

✿ If you are breast-feeding, rent a heavy-duty electric pump with a double pumping kit so that expressing takes less time. Double-expressing also helps stimulate the milk supply, and if you express from the very early days, you should be able to produce more than enough to feed both babies. Expressing milk earlier in the day also means that you can collect milk so that your partner can give the 10pm feed from a bottle.

✿ Do not feel guilty if you have to introduce some formula. It is better to do 80 per cent breast-feeding than attempt to do 100 per cent but give up because of exhaustion after a couple of weeks. If you are giving formula, try to do it at the 10pm feed rather than topping up at every feed during the day. If breast-feeding does not work, do not allow people to make you feel guilty. I know many sets of formula-fed twins who are growing up into very healthy and happy adults.

3
Weaning

Next to sleep, weaning is probably the most emotive subject in baby care. Between two and three months, just as you are beginning to see a regular pattern of milk feeding and sleep evolve, someone will bring up the subject of weaning. The baby will have discovered his hands, which can lead to endless sucking, chewing and dribbling. Well-meaning people will suggest that the baby is hungry and not satisfied on milk alone – but while this is a sign that a baby is ready to be weaned, it is by no means the only one. Do not be pressured into giving your baby solids until you are absolutely sure he is ready. It takes four months for the lining of the baby's gut to develop and the kidneys to mature enough to cope with the waste products from solid food. Solids before this time can have a damaging effect and may cause allergies. When you are sure that you and your baby are ready, you can begin. Remember, it is a gradual process, so don't hurry it. For a considerable time, milk will be the most important source of nutrition for your baby, so there is a while for you both to learn this new aspect of his growing up.

IS MY BABY READY FOR SOLIDS?

The World Health Organization now recommends that babies are exclusively breast-fed for six months. In the UK, the Department of Health acknowledges that all babies are different but advises that no solid food should be introduced earlier than 17 weeks. As a general guide, if your baby is at least four months old and weighs 5.5–6.5kg (12–14lb), he may be ready to begin taking a small amount of solids if he is showing most of the signs below. If your baby is under six months of age and showing all the signs of needing to be weaned, you should discuss your plans with your health visitor or GP.

❀ He has been feeding well and going four hours between feeds during the day, but now gets very irritable and chews his hand an hour or so before his next feed is due.

❀ He is bottle-fed and taking in more than 1,140ml (38oz) per day, but still appears hungry after a full feed four times a day.

❀ He usually sleeps well at night and at nap times, but is waking up earlier and earlier.

Important tips on introducing solids

✿ It is important to remember that babies under six months will still need at least four to five milk feeds a day – some may even need six. Solids before six months are tasters, not replacements.

✿ Introduce solids after the 11am feed so that your baby has had nearly half his daily intake of milk before noon, thus ensuring that he does not cut back on his milk intake too quickly.

✿ To avoid problems with the baby's digestion, introduce only one new food every three days.

✿ Studies have shown that a high-fruit diet for babies can lead to diarrhoea and slow growth, so keep the solids weighted towards baby rice and puréed vegetables. Too much fruit can also lead to a sweet tooth.

✿ All baby food must be salt free, and sugar used in only small quantities for stewing very sour fruit.

✿ Meat, chicken or fish should not be introduced until the baby is capable of digesting reasonable amounts of other solids, usually not until after six months of age.

✿ Dairy products, eggs, wheat, nuts and citrus foods should be avoided until after six months of age as they are likely to trigger allergies. If you have a history of allergies in your family, discuss when to introduce these foods with your health visitor.

* Symptoms of allergies include rashes, wheezing, coughing, runny nose, sore bottom, diarrhoea, irritability and swelling of the eyes. However, these symptoms can also be caused by house-mites, animal fur, wool and certain soaps and household cleaning agents, so don't leap to the wrong conclusion – consult your doctor.

* Honey should not be introduced before one year.

* Increase amounts of solid food gradually.

In my experience, babies introduced to a wide variety of foods in the early weaning stages will accept a wider range of foods at one year than those weaned on a restricted diet. I've also found that babies who are allowed excessive quantities of milk between four and six months and once weaned, are not encouraged to enjoy solids can end up as fussy eaters.

PREPARING TO INTRODUCE SOLIDS

Before you start introducing solids into your baby's diet, there are certain preparations and practices that you need to make second nature.

- When preparing food, ensure all surfaces are clean and wiped with anti-bacterial cleaner. Kitchen paper is more hygienic than cloths and towels.

- All fresh fruit and vegetables should be carefully peeled, and any core, pips and blemishes removed. They should be rinsed thoroughly with filtered water.

- All fruit and vegetables should be cooked by steaming or boiling in filtered water. Do not add salt, sugar or honey.

- Cook food until it is soft enough to be puréed to a very smooth consistency – similar to that of smooth yoghurt. A small amount of the cooking water may be needed.

- If using a food processor, check the mixture carefully for lumps by spooning or pouring it into another bowl. When lump-free, transfer to ice-cube trays or small containers for storage in the freezer.

- Freshly prepared food should be cooled and put in the fridge or freezer as soon as possible.

- Buy organic produce whenever possible, and avoid packet foods containing artificial flavourings, added sugars or fillers, such as maltodextrin.

- Food should be heated thoroughly to ensure that bacteria are killed.

- Make sure the food is cool enough before feeding it to your baby. Using a separate spoon, touch a small amount to your lips to check it is not too hot.

- Never feed straight from a jar – always transfer the contents to a dish. Leftovers should always be discarded.

- Arrange all the feed equipment in advance: baby chair, two bibs, two spoons and a clean, fresh, damp cloth.

- Use a shallow plastic spoon, never a metal one.

- Some babies need help learning how to feed from a spoon. Place the spoon just inside your baby's mouth and bring it up and out against the roof of his mouth so that his upper gums remove the food, encouraging him to feed.

- Always be positive and smile when offering new foods. If your baby spits something out, it may not mean that he dislikes it – simply that he is unfamiliar with it. If he positively refuses a food, leave it and try again in a week's time.

- Be guided by your baby as to when to increase amounts. Offer him the whole meal – he will turn his head away and get fussy when he has had enough. Increase the amounts once he is happy to eat everything you offer him and appears to want more.

✿ Encourage him to sit in his chair and entertain himself while you clear up. Any cloths and bibs should be put straight in to soak.

First stage of weaning

Suggested foods to introduce (4–6 months)

The following foods are all excellent first tastes of solids: baby rice, pear, apple, carrot, sweet potato, potato, green beans, courgettes and swede. Once your baby is happily taking these foods you can introduce the following: oats, parsnips, mango, peaches, broccoli, avocado, barley, peas, cauliflower.

If you are weaning your baby before six months you should introduce the foods every three days or so, increasing the amounts very gradually so that solids do not overtake the milk at this stage. If you have started weaning at six months you will need to work through the listed foods much more quickly and increase the amounts rapidly.

✿ During this stage, babies should taste cereal, plus a variety of fruit and vegetables.

- Food still needs to be puréed, but, between six and seven months, not so smoothly. This will prepare your baby for mashed food during the second stage.

- A baby may be ready to start having breakfast, once he shows signs of hunger long before his 11am feed. Organic oatmeal cereal with a small amount of puréed fruit seems to be a favourite with most babies.

- You should still give your baby most of his milk feed first.

- If your baby reaches seven months and shows no signs of wanting breakfast, it would be wise to reduce his milk feed very slightly and offer a small amount of solids.

- Your baby still needs a minimum of 600ml (20oz) of milk a day. Give milk feeds at breakfast, lunch, afternoon and evening, supplementing them with vegetable purée at lunch, and baby rice and fruit purée in the evening.

Second stage of weaning: up to 9 months

Suggested foods to introduce (from 6/7 to 9 months)
Between six and seven months your baby should have tasted most or all of the foods from the first stage weaning list. Provided you do not have a history of allergies in the family, wheat-based cereals,

pasta and bread can now be introduced. Fruit need not be cooked and puréed and can now simply be mashed. You can introduce fresh apricots, melon, plums and dried apricots, which have been soaked over-night, as well as well-diluted unsweetened fruit juices. Try to expand on the range of vegetables you are serving. Include coloured peppers, pumpkin, cabbage, and later spinach, Brussels sprouts and celery and tomatoes (provided there is no history of allergy). Meat, fish and pulses can be introduced. Use mild-tasting chicken, cod or haddock (not smoked) to begin with, then move on to lamb at seven to eight months. Red lentils, butter beans and other pulses can also be introduced at six months. Yoghurt and mild cheese (in cooking) can be included as well as first finger foods such as toast fingers, cooked carrot sticks or broccoli florets.

7 months

✿ Most babies are ready to accept stronger-tasting food at this age, and they will take pleasure from different textures, colours and presentation. Mash foods, but avoid mixing them together: keep different foods separate.

✿ From six months, once your baby is established on a variety of puréed foods, fruit can be raw but grated or mashed. Finger foods – soft fruit, lightly cooked vegetables and toast – can be introduced, but they will probably be sucked and squeezed rather than eaten. This is good training for later, though. Always wash your baby's hands before a meal and never leave him alone while he is eating.

✿ Your baby should be eating breakfast now – oat cereal mixed with fruit purée. Offer two-thirds of his milk feed first.

✿ Introducing a proper breakfast means that lunch can move on to between 11.45am and 12 noon. Chicken, fish and meat can be introduced at this stage, but do check that all bones are removed, and trim off any fat and skin. If the flavour is too strong on its own, try cooking chicken and meat in a casserole with some root vegetables, and fish in a milk sauce. Lentils or pulses are good alternatives to meat. Cow's milk can now be used in cooking but not as a drink. Watch for any adverse reactions.

✿ Once protein is introduced at lunchtime, replace the milk feed with a drink of water or well-diluted juice. Encourage your baby to start drinking from a beaker and offer most of the solids before the drink.

✿ At six months, your baby will have used up the store of iron he was born with, so it is important that he gets plenty of iron-rich food. To help improve iron absorption, serve cereals and meat with fruit or vegetables, and avoid giving milk with protein as it reduces the iron content by 50 per cent. If you have not weaned until six months you will need to move quickly through the food groups and introduce iron-rich foods as soon as possible.

✿ Your baby still needs 530–600ml (18–20oz) of milk a day, inclusive of milk used in food. Give milk feeds before breakfast, before lunch, in the afternoon and the evening, supplementing breakfast with, for example, oat cereal and fruit purée, lunch with potato or barley cereal and vegetables, and the evening feed with baby rice and fruit purée.

7–8 months

✿ You should now be ready to replace the solids offered after the 6pm milk feed with a proper tea at 5pm. This meal can consist of foods such as mini sandwiches, a baked potato or pasta served with vegetables and a sauce.

✿ Some babies get tired and fussy by teatime, so ensuring a well-balanced breakfast and lunch will take the strain off this meal. Try offering rice pudding or yoghurt if the baby does not eat much. Don't allow too large a drink at this meal as it will put him off his last milk feed.

✿ Your baby should now be ready to sit in his high chair for meals. If he has cut any teeth, they should be cleaned twice a day.

- Your baby should be eating 2–3 servings of carbohydrates a day in the form of cereal, wholemeal bread, pasta or potatoes. For information about what constitutes a serving see page 91.

- Cereal should be less refined now. Choose sugar-free ones rich in iron and vitamins, and serve with mashed fruit.

- Cheese should be full fat, pasteurised and grated.

- Your baby should have at least three servings of vegetables and fruit a day, and will also need one serving of animal or two of vegetable protein.

- By seven months start to mash solids so that the consistency is not quite so smooth, but without lumps. Once your baby has got used to eating food with slightly more texture, gradually mash it less and less until he will take food with lumps in it.

- You can introduce finger foods now if you haven't done so already. Rusks and toast can be offered if he is managing to eat cubes of raw soft fruit and cooked vegetables.

- Replace the lunchtime milk feed with water or well-diluted juice if the baby is eating protein.

- A very hungry baby may need a small drink and a piece of fruit mid-morning.

- Your baby still needs 530–600ml (18–20oz) of milk a day, inclusive of milk used in cooking. Milk feeds should be before breakfast, in the afternoon and at bedtime. Add cheese sauces, milk puddings and yoghurts if he is not taking enough.

* He should be eating three well-balanced meals a day and drinking three milk feeds a day, with his afternoon feed in a beaker. Well-diluted juice and water should also be offered in a beaker.

* Olive oil can be used in cooking and, by the end of eight months, small quantities of herbs.

* If the baby is refusing his last milk feed, try reducing his afternoon milk feed or replacing it with water. It is better to cut out milk in the afternoon than in the evening.

8–9 months

* As before, every day your baby should be eating 2–3 servings of carbohydrates, three servings of vegetables and fruit, one serving of animal protein or two of vegetable protein.

* Serve fruit and vegetables containing a high amount of vitamin C with protein meals: this aids iron absorption.

* Thoroughly wash and soak dried fruit, such as figs and prunes.

* Egg yolk can be introduced, but the egg should be hard-boiled.

- Avoid tuna in brine as the salt content is so high; choose tuna in spring water or vegetable oil instead.

- Your baby may show signs of wanting to feed himself. If so, use two spoons: load one for him to try himself, and the other to actually get the food in his mouth. Help his coordination by holding his wrist and gently guiding him.

- By the end of nine months, a bottle-fed baby should be taking all his breakfast milk from a beaker; add more milk and cheese-based sauces to his meals if he is losing interest in milk.

- Your baby still needs 530–600ml (18–20oz) of milk or formula a day, inclusive of milk used in cooking. Give milk feeds before breakfast and at bedtime.

Third stage of weaning: 9–12 months

Suggested foods to introduce

By this time your baby should be eating and enjoying all types of food, apart from those high in fat, salt or sugar. Stronger flavours, such as aubergine, beetroot, cucumber, fresh berries and high-fibre dried fruits such as prunes and figs, garlic, pineapple, small amounts of well-diluted unsweetened orange juice can be introduced. Beef and liver can be offered but only once a week and in small amounts. You can increase the range of herbs and spices used but again, use them in small amounts. Peanuts and honey, however, should still be avoided. It's important that your baby learns to chew properly at this stage: food should be chopped or diced, although meat still needs to be mashed or very finely chopped. This is also a good time to introduce raw vegetables and salads. Encourage your baby to learn to feed himself with finger food and his spoon, even if it tends to go all over the place at this stage. Never leave your baby alone while he is eating.

✿ Your baby should be enjoying three well-balanced meals a day and should be able to join in most of the family meals.

✿ The amount of teeth your baby has and how well he can chew will be a guide as to when to introduce tougher foods, such as beef and harder fruits.

✿ Every day your baby should be eating 3–4 servings of carbohydrates, such as cereal, wholemeal bread, pasta or potatoes; 3–4 portions of fruit and vegetables, including raw vegetables; one portion of animal protein and two of vegetable protein.

✿ At this stage he should be eating lots of finger foods, and his fruit and vegetables should be chopped and sliced rather than mashed.

✿ Try to make his meals look interesting and appealing. Do not overload his plate – serve a small amount and provide more when he has finished that. This can help to avoid the game of throwing food on the floor. If your baby does start to play up, refusing to eat and throwing his food on the floor, quietly and firmly say 'no' and remove the plate. Do not offer him a biscuit or fromage frais half an hour later, or he will soon learn that he will get something sweet if he plays up. A piece of fruit mid-afternoon will see him through to his tea.

❀ A drink of well-diluted, pure, unsweetened orange juice at lunch will aid iron absorption, but make sure that he has eaten most of his meal first.

❀ Some babies will cut out their afternoon milk feed altogether.

❀ By one year your baby will still need a minimum of 350ml (12oz) of milk split into two feeds, and inclusive of milk used in food. If he isn't drinking enough, give him extra cheese and yoghurt.

❀ It is important that large volumes of milk are discouraged by this stage. No more than 600ml (20oz), inclusive of milk used in food, should be allowed.

❀ Cow's milk can be introduced as a drink from the age of one year – it should be full fat, pasteurised and preferably organic (research has shown that organic milk contains less mucus).

❀ Avoid sweet and salty snacks, such as biscuits, cakes and crisps.

HELP!

Not every child will take smoothly and easily to solids, and you are bound to run into an obstacle or two along the way. Indeed, you are very lucky if you do not! Don't worry, though – there are solutions to most eating dilemmas. Here are some common problems and remedies.

Refusing solids

❀ Babies aged six months or older often refuse solids because they drink too much milk, especially if they are still feeding in the middle of the night. Milk is still the most important food for babies under six months, but the introduction of solids can be affected if feeds aren't structured.

❀ If your baby is six months, taking five full milk feeds a day and refusing solids, I would suggest you ask your health visitor about gradually reducing one of the milk feeds to encourage his interest in solids. If he has to be woken at 7am, I would advise cutting back gradually on the 10pm feed; if he is waking earlier than 7am, I suggest that you cut back on the 11am milk feed instead so as to encourage him to take solids then. Once he is happy taking solids at 11am, introduce some at the 6pm feed. As his appetite increases, so will the amount of solids he takes, which will have the knock-on effect of him drinking less at the 10pm feed.

✿ By the end of six months, a baby's milk intake should be around 600ml (20oz) a day, divided between three drinks a day and small amounts used in food. If your baby still refuses solids at this age, despite cutting down on his milk intake, it is important that you discuss the problem with your doctor or health visitor.

Refusing milk

✿ The amount of milk a six-month-old baby drinks will gradually begin to reduce as his intake of solid food increases. However, up to the age of nine months a baby still needs a minimum of 530–600ml (18–20oz) a day of breast or formula milk. This daily amount gradually reduces to a minimum of 350ml (12oz) at one year of age. If your baby is losing interest or refusing some of his milk feeds and taking less than the recommended amounts, careful attention should be given to the timing of solids and the type of food given.

✿ Up to the age of six months a baby should still be taking a full milk feed morning and evening. A full milk feed consists of 210–240ml (7–8oz) or a feed from both breasts. Babies under six months who are given solids in the middle of their milk feed will be more likely to refuse the remainder of their formula or the second breast.

* A baby under five months of age still needs a full milk feed at 11am, even if he is being weaned early. Introducing breakfast too soon, or offering too much solid food first thing in the morning, can cause a baby to cut down too quickly or to refuse the 11am feed.

* The 11am milk feed should be reduced gradually between the ages of five and six months. Introducing the tier system of feeding (milk, solids, milk) before five months can also be the reason a baby refuses his milk at this feed.

* Giving lunchtime solids at 2pm and evening solids at 5pm is the reason many babies under six months cut down too quickly or refuse their 6pm feed. Until he reaches six months it is better to give a baby his lunchtime solids at 11am and his evening solids after he has had a full milk feed at 6pm.

* Giving hard-to-digest foods, such as banana or avocado, at the wrong time of day can cause a baby to cut back on the next milk feed. Until a baby reaches six months it is better to serve these types of food after the 6pm feed rather than during the day.

* Babies over six months of age who begin to refuse milk are often being allowed too many snacks in between meals or too much

juice. Try replacing juice with water and cutting out snacks in between meals.

✿ Between nine and 12 months some babies begin refusing the bedtime milk feed, which is a sign that they are ready to drop their third milk feed. If this happens, it is important to reduce the amount given at the afternoon feed before eventually dropping it altogether.

Fussy feeding in the first year

If milk feeding is structured properly during the early days of weaning, the majority of babies will happily eat most of the foods they are offered. By the time they reach nine months, babies should be getting most of their nourishment from eating three solid meals a day. Parents are advised to offer their babies a wide variety of foods to ensure that they receive all the nutrients they need. However, it is often around this time that many babies start to reject food they have previously enjoyed. If your baby is between nine and 12 months of age and suddenly starts to reject his food, or becomes fussy and fretful at mealtimes, the following guidelines should help determine the cause.

✿ Parents can have unrealistic expectations of the amounts of food their baby can eat, and serving over-large portions can mislead them into thinking that their baby has a feeding problem. See the recommended quantities below.

Amounts needed at 9–12 months

3–4 servings of carbohydrates, made up of cereal, wholemeal bread, pasta or potatoes. 1 tablespoon of cereal or half a small baked potato.

3–4 servings of fruit and vegetables, including raw vegetables. A serving is one small apple, pear, banana or carrot, a couple of cauliflower or broccoli florets or two tablespoons of chopped green beans.

1 serving of animal protein or two of vegetable protein. A serving is 1 tablespoon of poultry, meat or fish, or 3 tablespoons of pulses (lentils, peas, beans).

✿ Self-feeding plays an important role in a baby's mental and physical development as it encourages hand-to-eye coordination and increases his sense of independence. Between six and nine months of age most babies will start to pick up their food and try to feed themselves. This can be very messy and make mealtimes take much longer, but restricting a baby's natural desire to explore his food and feed himself will only lead to frustration and very often a refusal to be spoon-fed. Introducing lots of finger foods and allowing him to eat part of his meal by himself, regardless of the mess he makes, will make him much more inclined to take the remainder from you off a spoon.

✿ By the time a baby reaches nine months of age he will become more interested in the colour, shape and texture of his food. A baby who is still having all the different foods mashed up together will quickly begin to get bored with even his favourite foods, and this is one of the main reasons that babies lose interest in vegetables.

✿ Offering your baby a selection of vegetables of various textures and colours at each meal in small amounts will be more appealing to him than a large amount of just one or two vegetables.

✿ Sweet puddings and ice-cream served on a regular basis are a major cause of babies and toddlers refusing their main course. Even babies as young as nine months can quickly learn that if they refuse the savoury foods and fuss enough, they will more than likely be given the pudding. It is better to restrict puddings and desserts to special occasions, and serve your baby fresh fruit, yoghurt or cheese as a second course.

❀ If your baby rejects a particular food, it is important that he should be offered it again a couple of weeks later. Babies' likes and dislikes regarding food fluctuate a good deal in the first year, and parents who don't persist with trying rejected foods often find that their baby ends up eating a very restricted diet.

❀ Giving large amounts of juice or water before a meal can stop a baby feeding well. Try to offer him drinks midway between meals, not an hour before. At mealtimes, encourage him to eat at least half of the solids before offering him a drink of water or well-diluted juice.

❀ The timing of meals also plays a big part in how well a baby eats. A baby who is having his breakfast solids later than 8am is unlikely to be very hungry for his lunch much before 1pm. Likewise, a baby who is having teatime solids later than 5pm may be getting too tired to eat well.

❀ Hard-to-digest snacks, such as bananas or cheese, can often take the edge off a baby's appetite. Try restricting snacks for a couple of days to see if his appetite improves at mealtimes.

❀ If you are concerned that your baby is not taking enough solids, seek advice from your health visitor or doctor. Keep a diary for a week, listing the times and amounts of all food and drink consumed, as this will help them to determine the cause of your baby's feeding problems.

Fussy feeding in the second year

During the second year, many toddlers develop an erratic feeding pattern. Some days they will eat three good meals, on others just one, and some days they will want to eat all day. This is very common, and it's vital that you do not start to cajole, bribe or try to force your child to eat. The important thing is that your toddler's nutritional needs are being met over a period of several days. Mealtimes must not become a battle of wills. In my experience, toddlers who are going through a fussy stage and who are constantly coaxed, bribed or force-fed by spoon nearly always end up with a long-term eating problem.

Tips for dealing with fussy toddlers

✿ Set rules and boundaries and try to stick to them so that the child's erratic eating pattern does not become a real problem.

✿ Keep a food diary listing all the foods and drinks that your toddler consumes and at what times. If you find that he is actually eating a lot less than the recommended amounts over several days, you should discuss things with your doctor or health visitor.

* Make a note of your toddler's behaviour at mealtimes and whether you think his lack of appetite could have been caused by over-tiredness or overexcitement.

* Snacks and drinks should be given midway between meals so that they do not take the edge off your toddler's appetite.

* Choose healthy snacks that are not too filling – fresh and dried fruit or raw chopped vegetables are excellent. Try not to offer too much cheese or banana, which take time to digest.

* Fruit juice can reduce the appetite, so encourage your child to drink water in between meals, and offer well-diluted juice no later than two hours before meals.

* Too much milk is one of the main causes of toddlers refusing to eat or becoming fussy about eating. Your toddler still needs a minimum of 350ml (12oz) a day and a maximum of 500ml (17oz) a day. This should be divided between two or three milk feeds a day, inclusive of milk used in food. Cut back on milk if your toddler is taking in too much.

* If your toddler starts to refuse his milk or takes less than the minimum daily requirement, increase the amount used in cereals,

sauces and healthy puddings. Offer extra yoghurt, fromage frais, cheese and dark green leafy vegetables, which are high in calcium.

* Try small quantities of different foods rather than large quantities of one or two foods.

* Make food look attractive; offer two or three different coloured vegetables at mealtimes.

* Keep foods separate at this stage, rather than mixed together, so that your toddler becomes aware of different shapes, colours and textures.

* At mealtimes encourage your toddler to eat at least half of his food before offering juice or water.

* Avoid feeding your toddler when he is overtired.

* Finish breakfast by 8am so that he is hungry for lunch at 12 noon, thus ensuring that he is ready for a good tea around 5pm.

* Give mid-morning snacks around 9.30–10am and mid-afternoon snacks no later than 3pm.

* Establish regular mealtimes and avoid distractions, such as television or playing games.

* Do not force, cajole or bribe your toddler with puddings or sweets as an incentive to eat his main course. If he starts to mess around with his food or become fussy, remove the food immediately

without making any comment about his not eating, then try to make him wait until his next scheduled meal or snack time.

✿ Avoid foods high in sugar, starch and fillers as they can cause loss of appetite. These include tinned foods, such as baked beans, soup and fruit, and some leading brands of fromage frais, which can have as much as 14.5g (three teaspoons) of sugar in a 100g pot. Check the labels for lists of ingredients.

✿ Try to serve your toddler the same foods as the rest of the family, cutting them into bite-size pieces.

✿ Encourage your toddler to self-feed and try not to show signs of being overfussy about the mess.

✿ During the second year many toddlers are very tired by the end of the day, so make teatime relaxed and easy. Try to give your toddler his main protein meal of the day at lunchtime so that tea can be something quick and easy to prepare, such as pasta or a thick soup with sandwiches.

Further weaning information, along with lots of recipes, is available in *The Contented Little Baby Book of Weaning*.

4
Potty Training

Potty training requires good humour, patience and encouragement, but I believe that if it's handled sensibly, successful training can be achieved in a very short time. The main thing is not to start too soon. Unless a child can control his bladder and bowel movements, you are not going to achieve really successful potty training. The more experienced the mother or carer, the more likely it is that she will wait for the child to be more than ready, thus avoiding the accidents, wet clothes and frustration that go with unsuccessful potty training.

The biggest problems happen when the mother, either through misplaced enthusiasm or peer pressure, begins potty training too soon. I have heard of childminders putting nine-month-old babies on the potty, and mothers-in-law insisting that their offspring was potty trained at 12 months. Yet trying to train a child who is not ready can lead to ongoing problems, and upset for both the child and the carer. It does not harm a child to be older than is ideal, and in my experience, children aged 2½–3 can be potty trained in as little as 48 hours since their understanding and bladder control is then so much more advanced. I know that some nurseries request that two and half-year-olds should be potty trained on arrival, but it is important to remember that all children are different.

I also encourage mothers to try to plan potty training when the weather is warmer. Of course, this not always possible, but there is no doubt that potty training a child when he or she can be outside without a nappy on has clear advantages. Also late spring, summer and early autumn clothes tend to be lighter and quicker to pull on and off than tights and thick trousers.

Indications that your child is ready for potty training

* He is over 18 months of age.
* He has a dry nappy for more than a couple of hours (this indicates that he is getting some bladder control), and his nappy is frequently dry when you get him up from his lunchtime nap.

- He is aware when he is doing a poo, perhaps by going very quiet and showing signs of concentration, or he points to his nappy and says 'poo' or 'pee pee' when he has done one.

- He can understand and follow simple instructions, such as 'Go and fetch your red ball' or 'Put your toy in the box'.

- He is eager to participate in taking off his own clothes, shoes, socks and shorts, and understands what pulling his shorts up and down means.

- He can point to the different parts of his body when you name them.

- He has the ability to sit still and occupy himself or concentrate for 5–10 minutes with a toy, book or video.

Tips for cooperation with potty training

✿ Encourage your child to participate in tasks such as dressing and undressing and helping to tidy his toys away.

✿ Use a star chart as an incentive for a child who does not willingly perform these tasks. Mark a cross in a box every time you request your child to do something, and if he cooperates, cover the cross with a sticker. Once you see several consecutive days where nearly all the crosses are covered with a sticker, you can be confident that your child is ready to cooperate with potty training.

Equipment needed for potty training

✿ Two potties

✿ Child's toilet seat

✿ Cushion for use in the buggy or when travelling (cover a thin cushion with a polythene bag and then a washable cover)

✿ About 8–10 pairs of pants

✿ Selection of storybooks, cassette tapes and videos

- ❋ Star chart – make your own, then buy stickers from stationery shops or supermarkets
- ❋ Facecloths for drying hands on
- ❋ Booster step
- ❋ Two buckets

Potty training is best avoided when . . .

- ❋ Either a new baby is due within a couple of months or has arrived within the last couple of months. My advice to expectant mothers whose elder child is ready for potty training is to wait until the baby is at least four months old. A toddler quickly realises the immediate effect it has on those around him to shout, 'I need a poo!' or 'Pee pee coming!' He will soon begin to use this as a means of getting attention if there is a new baby in the house taking up Mummy and Daddy's time.

- ❋ You have just moved or are about to move house.

- ❋ Your child has recently recovered from an illness.

- ❋ There has been a change in childcare circumstances.

- ❋ You or your partner are experiencing pressure at work.

- Either older or younger siblings are going through sleeping difficulties or behavioural problems.

- Times such as Christmas and holidays, when lots of social activities are planned.

POTTY TRAINING – STAGE 1

At this stage you want to familiarise your child with the potty and get him happy to sit on it for several minutes at a time. Learning the difference between wet and dry is also important.

Introducing the potty

- Once your child is showing all the signs of readiness, put a potty in the bathroom. The first step would be to take him to the bathroom as much as possible and encourage him to sit on his potty, but do not bother removing his nappy at this stage. Allowing him to watch you demonstrate while you describe clearly and simply what you are doing will help teach your child in advance what will eventually be expected of him.

- If you have an older child, cousin or small friend in the house, ask him or her to pretend to use the potty for the benefit of your toddler. This helps your child familiarise himself with its use. Children love to copy older children and bigger siblings.

✿ When you wash your hands, encourage him to join in, washing and drying his own hands at the same time as you are doing yours. Place a lot of emphasis on the words wet and dry, demonstrating how his hands become wet with water when washed, and then dry when wiped with the towel.

✿ When you begin training and your child is wearing pants, it is extremely important never to show signs of anger, disgust or disapproval when dealing with his accidents. Do not say things such as, 'Oh, you naughty boy, what smelly wet knickers' or 'What a stinky poo'. Some young children are very sensitive about their bodily functions and take any disapproval of their pee or poo as a personal rejection.

✿ Deal sensitively with accidents, and remember to give lots of encouragement, even if early attempts are unsuccessful.

✿ Let your child choose some 'big boy' Action Man pants, or for a girl some pretty knickers to encourage a feeling of excitement in taking this step in their development.

✿ If your child is happy to participate when you take him with you to the bathroom and shows all the other signs of readiness for potty training, you can move on to the next part of this first stage.

✿ He should be encouraged to sit on his potty without his nappy while you prepare his bath. Five to 10 minutes is long enough, and if he manages to do anything in the potty, remember to give him lots of praise.

❀ When praising your child it is important that he understands why you are pleased with him. For example, say how clever he is at sitting on his potty, or how clever he is at peeing in his potty.

❀ Try to avoid saying what a good boy he is, as he may start to think he is bad if he doesn't manage to make it to the potty.

❀ Once he is happy to sit on the potty at bathtime, you should try sitting him on it after breakfast when he is changing out of his pyjamas and when you get him up from his nap. Again the nappy should be taken off and he should be encouraged to sit for a short spell on his potty. Don't worry if he doesn't manage to do anything – this is just practising.

❀ Many children are clean before they are dry because it is easier for them to control their bowel than their bladder. If your child does a poo around the same time every day, try sitting him on the potty at that time. It can be a bit hit and miss at this stage: sometimes he may do it in the potty, other times he will do it the minute you put his nappy on. Give him lots of praise if he does poo in the potty, but do not scold him or show disapproval if he does it in his nappy. Encouragement and gentle reassurance that he will probably do it in the potty the next time will get better results in the long term.

✿ Some children will start to hold back from doing a poo when the potty is first introduced; they will go two or three days, then do it in their nappy. Do not put pressure on the child if this happens, as it will only make matters worse. Increase the amount of fruit and vegetables he eats, and offer extra fluid to help avoid the problem of constipation.

✿ Once he is happy sitting on the potty at the previously mentioned times over a period of at least a week, you can consider the next stage of potty training.

POTTY TRAINING – STAGE 2

It is very important to choose a week that is fairly free of activities, especially for the first couple of days. Explain to family and friends that you are potty training, so you will be unavailable for telephone calls and visits during the daytime. If you have other children, it is probably better to start at the weekend, when your partner can help out. To train your toddler quickly and successfully, it is very important not only that you are in a relaxed state of mind, but that any older or younger siblings are happy and in a good enough routine to allow 100 per cent concentration and the extra time needed to achieve this. Your toddler will need your constant attention and encouragement during the first couple of days, otherwise he will very quickly lose interest.

For the first day or two you might find it easier to allow your child to run around without any pants or trousers, but remember that the whole concept of potty training is for the child to learn the difference between wet and dry, and this is much easier to achieve when he is wearing pants. It also means that when accidents happen indoors, most of the pee is soaked up into the pants and not the carpet.

* During the first few days, try to restrict training to just a couple of rooms. I suggest starting off the first morning of training in the kitchen so that you can keep a close eye on the child while you are doing the chores.

* Involve the child in things such as washing up or baking so that he doesn't get bored, and if accidents happen, they are easily cleaned up.

* When moving to another room with carpets, put the potty on an old rug or a thick, doubled-up towel. Accidents almost always happen near the potty when the child didn't get there quite quickly enough.

* It is essential to teach your child the importance of proper hygiene and hand washing from the very start of potty training. The use of novelty soaps and cartoon-illustrated hand cloths can help make hand washing and drying more fun.

* It is important to help children practise how to wipe their bottoms (girls from front to back) and how to wash their hands thoroughly.

* It might be a good idea to invite friends over for your child to prevent him from getting bored. It is even better if his friend is potty trained, as he will more than likely be keen to show off his potty and big-boy pants.

Day 1

* Put your toddler straight into his special big-boy pants, but leave trousers, shoes and socks off for the first couple of days.

* Talk positively, explaining that he is a big boy now and can wear pants like Mummy and Daddy and he can use his potty.

* Continue taking him to the bathroom with you and explaining what you are doing. Suggest that he sits on his potty at the same time so you can both do a pee together.

* Try to be relaxed and positive; do not show disapproval or disappointment when he has an accident. Emphasise how clever he

is sitting on his potty and wearing big-boy pants like Mummy and Daddy.

❀ The length of time it takes for a child to use the potty several times successfully varies from child to child. Some children are peeing regularly in the potty within a couple of hours; with others it can take several hours, and there have been a few where it has been well into the second day before any reasonable results are achieved. Do not despair if your child wets his pants several times before he manages to do it in the potty. Once he does manage to pee in it a couple of times in a row, he will be so proud of himself that he will be very keen to keep showing you his new skill.

❀ When he is successful at using the potty, tell him how clever he is at peeing in the potty and how happy and proud you are. Lots of praise, hugs and applause along with the use of a star chart are the most effective ways of encouraging him to continue using the potty.

❀ When explaining to your child what is expected of him, it is important that you get down to his level so that you have eye-to-eye contact. Never shout instructions across the room and assume that he has taken in what you have said.

❀ Try to have a variety of different activities planned throughout the day. Drawing, jigsaws, collages and anything that can be done at the kitchen table is a good idea. Try to save reading stories and watching videos for times when he appears not to be so interested in using a potty. If he has gone a couple of hours without doing a pee, encourage him to sit on his potty and read him a story, or sit with him and watch a video for a short spell.

✿ As the day progresses, you should gradually go from reminding him to sit on the potty, to taking him if he needs to use it. It is important for his mental and physical awareness that you start to allow him some responsibility for deciding when he needs to use the potty, even if it means occasional accidents.

✿ Keep a record of when he needs the potty. If you can see a particular pattern occurring on your chart, you should be able to use it to tell when to go from suggesting that he sits on his potty to reminding him where it is if he needs to use it.

✿ The point to remember on Day 1 is that it is not important how many times your child pees in the potty. The most important thing is that he is happy to sit on it for short spells at regular intervals throughout the day.

✿ Do not get despondent if your child has lots of accidents. A couple of pees in the potty by the end of the first day is fine.

Day 2

* Some children seem to have endless accidents the first couple of days, and then suddenly it all falls into place by the third day. These mishaps can actually help your child to become more aware of his need to pee, and of the difference between wet and dry. As before, do not make a fuss or scold your toddler if he has an accident: simply remind him what the potty is for.

* Make sure that the activities you arrange are not too boisterous – it could lead to your child becoming overexcited and forgetting about the potty altogether.

* If your child is playing outdoors, it is important to take the potty out with you and put it in a prominent place. It often helps if you let your child decide where he would like it to be put.

* By the end of the second day you should begin to feel that you are getting somewhere with potty training and that your child is grasping what is expected of him.

* Consistency is of the utmost importance if you want to potty train quickly and successfully. Dress your toddler in pants at all times during the day – nappies are for sleep times only.

Day 3 – Going out

The following tips should help when you and your child have to go out or take a car journey.

* In the early days it is advisable to take a couple of changes of clothes and pants on outings, plus a plastic bag to hold any wet items. Remember your child's special cushion when travelling in the car or using the buggy.

* Don't be tempted to put him back into nappies or trainer pants when travelling. This will only confuse your child, and I've found that flitting back and forth from pants to nappies is one of the main reasons why potty training can take so long for many parents to achieve.

* Before you leave the house take your child and his potty with you to the bathroom, explain that you are going to sit on the loo and do a pee, and that he should sit on his potty as well. Encourage him to sit for 5–10 minutes by reading him a story.

* Some parents report that running the cold tap while sitting the child on the potty often encourages him to do a pee. It will do no harm to try this if nothing has happened within five minutes.

* Once 10 minutes have elapsed, I would not insist that he sit any longer. I would prepare for the outing, which should ideally be

only a 10-minute journey, and trust to luck that you get there without any accidents.

✿ Until your child is used to the big loo and confident about using it, you will need to take his potty with you. There are travel potties available, but unless you plan to do lots of long journeys, it is probably not worth buying one. With any luck, your child will be used to using the big loo regularly within a couple of weeks of being trained.

Days 4–7

✿ By the end of the first week you should aim towards getting your child used to going to the bathroom when he needs to do a pee or a poo. Over the next few days the potty should gradually be moved nearer and nearer to the bathroom. Once your toddler shows signs that he can control his bladder long enough to get to the bathroom, it should remain there permanently.

✿ If a couple of hours have gone by without him using the potty, and he seems particularly engrossed in something, it would be advisable to remind him where the potty is.

✿ Try not to nag him about it; it is much better to allow him to take the lead at this stage and to have the odd accident, than end up in a situation where he becomes dependent on your reminding him or, worse, rebels totally against potty training because he feels under constant pressure.

✿ Once you have established that the bathroom is where he does a pee and a poo, you can now encourage him to use the big loo. The sooner the child is encouraged to use the big loo, the less likely he is to become frightened of it.

✿ Always use one of the specially designed seats that fit over the loo, then get down to his level and hold him on the loo under his arms until he becomes more confident about holding on to the handles of the child seat. He may also feel more confident if you have a little step for him to rest his feet on.

✿ You could ask either his grandparents or one of his favourite aunts to send him a special loo seat as a reward for being such a clever boy at wearing his pants. By making the loo seat appear as a reward, he will be much more accepting of it.

✿ It is important to be very gentle when putting him on the loo seat, so reassure him that you will kneel down and stay right beside him until he has finished. He may still wish to use his potty some of the time, but do try to get him to use both the potty and the big loo by the end of the first week.

✿ His star chart and stickers can be used as an incentive to use the big loo. Buy some extra big stars to put on the chart for when he uses the big loo. If he has more than three big stars on his chart by teatime, he could be given a treat of an ice-cream or his favourite biscuit after his tea.

✿ The majority of toddlers are dry most of the time by the end of the first week, with only the occasional accident.

✿ Finally, it is important to remember that most children under three years of age will continue to have the occasional accident, particularly if they are overexcited during play, or overtired. While it is important not to get angry or punish them, I would insist that they help to clear up any mess so that they learn that peeing or pooing anywhere other than the potty or loo has its consequences.

Night-times and nap times

✿ I would continue to put a toddler in nappies during his daytime sleep until his nappy has been consistently dry on waking for at least two weeks. After that I would feel confident that it is safe to abandon it.

✿ For the night-time sleep, continue with nappies for several months. In my experience, very few children are capable of going through the night without wetting before the age of three years, and with boys it may be even later. Pushing night-time training before this age often means ending up with other problems. One major problem is that if the nappy is abandoned too early, it is usually necessary either to install a night-light or to leave the door slightly ajar so that the child can see his way to the potty or loo. With toddlers under three years, the temptation to start running around in the middle of the night is often too hard to resist, especially if they know Mummy is attending to a younger sibling.

✿ With a child over three years who is consistently dry and clean, I would explain that he no longer needs to wear a nappy at night, and make sure that he goes on the potty just before he gets into bed so that he shouldn't need to pee during the night. If you find that he starts to wake up in the night needing his potty, at this age he should be capable of getting out of bed and using the potty himself. Obviously, you would then have to install a small, low-voltage night-light in his room.

✿ If night-time accidents occur, there are special waterproof pads that can be placed across the middle of the bed. If your child is one of the few who does not like the feel of these pads, use a waterproof sheet, then a further pad, such as a folded sheet, and finally a fitted sheet. This way, if your child does have an accident in the night, you can simply whip away the first two layers and avoid having to remake the bed completely.

✿ Finally, remember that your child should not have excessive drinks before bedtime. A cup of milk should be given no later than 6pm, and if he is still thirsty at bedtime, offer a small amount of water.

POTTY TRAINING TWINS

Do not attempt to train twins together if one is showing signs of readiness and the other isn't. Train the one who is showing all the signs, but try to get someone else to care for the other twin for part of the day. This helps avoid possible distractions and prevents the child who isn't ready being made to feel guilty.

As long as there is no pressure on the second twin to use the potty, he will eventually start to use it of his own accord in a very short space of time.

Tips for potty training twins

✿ Do not rush into potty training too quickly; wait until the twins are at least two years of age.

- It is often easier to potty train them separately, particularly if they have older or younger siblings.

- Have a potty of the same design and colour for each child so that they do not fight over the same potty.

- If potty training both children, be careful not to compare them against each other. It should not become so competitive that one of the children begins to feel pressurised.

- Have more pants and facecloths than the recommended amount so that you are not under pressure if you get behind with the laundry.

5
Behaviour and Habits

One thing that all parents want for their baby is that he grows up to be a happy, healthy and confident adult. During the growing years, most parents hope to raise a child who is polite, well mannered, content and generous of spirit. It's a tall order for such a little person, and one look around the average nursery or children's party will show you that not everyone is succeeding as well as they would like. Toddlers can be strong-willed, self-centred and prone to temper tantrums – it seems that nature designed them that way – but there are things you can do to help your child become contented and confident. I do not claim to have the golden solution that guarantees a perfect child, but over the years of working and living with many families all over the world, I've observed enough baby and toddler behaviour to formulate some ways of dealing with children. Of course, all children are different, and some will respond to methods that simply bounce off others, but here are some of the ways to set your child on the path to becoming a contented little person.

PLAYTIME AND KEEPING YOUR CHILD AMUSED

Very young babies spend the waking hours of their first few weeks feeding, burping and being changed, but by the third week, they are beginning to become more alert and aware of their surroundings. Even at this early stage, they can benefit from social activity and visual stimulation. This can be both an amusement and an aid to brain development, as well as encouraging babies to learn to entertain themselves.

Toys for babies under six months old

❋ A musical mobile hung above the cot will give hours of amusement to a young baby, and help develop his eye muscles as he follows the moving objects. Choose one that is brightly coloured and interesting to look at from underneath. Faces of animals and clowns are always great favourites. Remember to remove the mobile from the cot when your baby goes to sleep.

- A baby gym is a frame with a variety of toys hanging from it, and the baby lies underneath it. Alternatively, the baby can lie on an activity mat that has toys attached to it; this can be folded up when not in use. Both gyms and mats come in an assortment of styles and colours, but the black, red and white versions seem to captivate babies' attention the most. A baby gym will encourage your baby to kick and develop his hand-eye coordination as he tries to grab the dangling toys. A very small baby may be more comfortable if a travel rug is placed on the floor under the baby gym.

- Black and white cloth books are always popular with young babies. They can be secured along the side of the cot or pram, or hung near the changing table so that the baby can see them while being massaged after the bath or when he is having his nappy changed.

- Other books that show colourful single objects or faces will be popular. Even very young babies will show an interest in simple lift-the-flap books, such as *Spot the Dog*.

- Fabric rattles that are soft and light to handle are very popular with babies over four months. Choose brightly coloured ones with smiling faces.

- A baby mirror is another toy that babies seem to love. Some have a mirror on one side and a black, white and red design on the reverse.

✿ There are various colourful soft toys designed to squeak, rattle or rustle. These are usually made from different types of fabric, encouraging an awareness of texture. The most popular ones are an octopus, a snake and a clown that wobbles.

✿ Babies of all ages will benefit from hearing different types of music, and they enjoy being danced with. There are also many classes that they seem to enjoy, including massage, swimming and baby gym. Check with your local library for details of classes in your area.

✿ Toys and classes are not the only way to relieve your baby's boredom: even the youngest will enjoy the atmosphere, noise and activity of a trip to the local museum, art gallery and even the supermarket.

Toys for babies over six months old

Babies over six months can get particularly frustrated and bored. Unlike younger babies, they will not be content to lie for 20 minutes or so under the cot mobile or on the activity mat. The toys listed below are some that are popular with older babies. (Always check that they conform to British standard BS5665.)

* Colourful balls are a great hit with older babies. Some have several buttons that, when pressed, make different sounds. Others are clear, with an object inside that wobbles when the ball is rolled.

* Activity centres that fix to the side of the cot or playpen are designed to help develop a baby's manual skills. They have a selection of dials, buttons and bells that make different sounds, and some incorporate a musical device. The one that is designed to look like a teddy bear is very popular.

* Baby bouncers that are suspended from a door or special frame are excellent for older babies who have enough neck control to support their heads.

* Soft toys, such as snakes, crocodiles and birds, that are designed to squeak, crinkle, rattle and make different noises are great for a multi-sensory experience.

* Stacker toys, composed of different stackable shapes, will help develop your baby's hand and wrist control. Choose brightly coloured ones, where each shape has a different texture and makes a different sound.

* Be careful to avoid overstimulation. I find it helps to have quiet toys and soft books for the wind-down period before a nap or

bedtime, and to keep noisy games, toys and high-level stimulation for the baby's wakeful, social time.

ANXIETY

It is quite normal for babies to become more clingy between six and nine months because it is now that they begin to realise they are separate from their mothers. A previously easygoing baby can suddenly become demanding and upset if his mother leaves the room. All babies go through this to some extent, and it is important to understand that they are not being naughty or demanding. Forcing your baby to go to strangers, or leaving him alone in a room to play by himself, will not solve the problem, and may lead him to become more fretful and insecure. Responding quickly and positively to his anxiety rather than ignoring it will, in the long run, help him become more confident and independent.

Although this stage can be very exhausting for a mother, it rarely lasts long. The following tips can help make this difficult period less stressful.

✿ Many babies develop a need for a comforter at this age, usually a special blanket, cloth or toy.

✿ If you are planning to return to work when your baby is between six and nine months, it is important to make sure that he gets accustomed to being left with someone else before he reaches that age.

* Get him used to the nursery or childminder at least two weeks before returning to work. Gradually lengthen the period of time you leave him.

* Provided you are confident that your baby is happy with his carer, do not prolong the goodbye. A hug and a kiss, and a reminder that you will be back soon, are enough. Using the same approach and words each time will, in the long term, be more reassuring than going back to try and calm him.

* During this period ask your baby's carer not to subject him to too many different new things at once or too much handling by strangers. The calmer and more predictable his routine, the quicker he will get over his feeling of anxiety.

* Try to arrange regular play dates with just a small group of the same mothers and babies. Once he appears to be happier and begins responding to the familiar faces, gradually introduce him to larger groups and to other new experiences.

FROM BABY TO TODDLER

The key development during a child's transition from baby to toddler is that he becomes mobile. The majority of babies begin to take their first steps just before their first birthday, and these signify the beginning of the journey into toddlerhood. Once he is walking, your child's perception of the world around him suddenly changes, and his curiosity increases as he views more things from an upright level. This newfound mobility is a vital stage in a toddler's development, as it gives him the independence to explore his surroundings, and the ability to acquire other skills. He learns more between the ages of one and three than at any other time of his life. The learning process often ends up in tears of frustration through not being understood, and sheer exhaustion from having to learn so many different things at the same time. This time often sees the arrival of a new baby, which adds the fear of abandonment and feelings of jealousy to the very long list of emotions with which the toddler is having to cope.

Main skills and challenges for toddlers

✿ Learning to make his needs understood – by talking.

✿ Learning to become more physically independent – by walking, undressing and dressing himself.

- ✿ Learning how to make choices about what to eat and how to feed himself.

- ✿ Learning bladder and bowel control – by potty training.

- ✿ Learning how to integrate with other toddlers – by playing and sharing.

- ✿ Learning how to become less dependent on his parents – by attending playgroup or nursery.

During this stage of development it is essential that a toddler has a safe, happy and relaxed environment to master these skills confidently. Toddlers soon become very frustrated if they keep hearing the word 'no', or are constantly reminded to be careful or not to touch. Try to toddler-proof your home, or at least one room of it, so that your child can play happily and freely without the risk of hurting himself (see Chapter 6 for further tips). It is important that his natural curiosity is not hampered by constant nagging to be careful with Mummy's pot plants or not to get any dirty fingerprints on the white paintwork. There will be times when your toddler becomes so challenged that he finds it difficult to cope, and it is essential that parents set very clear limits and boundaries for dealing with any difficult behaviour caused by their toddler's frustration. Some of the tips below will help with your toddler's basic development.

Walking

While the majority of toddlers are walking after their first birthday, it can take several more months of practice to achieve the balance and coordination needed for steady walking. Before that, they do not have the ability to steer themselves properly, so there will be much falling over and bumping into things, which can lead to frustration and tantrums. Here are some suggestions to help make things easier for your toddler during the early stages of walking.

❀ Toddlers will find it easier to learn to walk if they go barefoot, as splaying their toes fully enables them to get a better grip. It is also better for muscle tone and the development of the feet. In very cold weather it is better for them to wear socks with non-slip soles when walking indoors as even the softest shoes can restrict foot growth.

❀ The first toddling steps are often referred to as 'cruising'. A toddler will begin to walk sideways first. He uses both hands to pull himself up and hold on to the furniture and support himself as he moves around. Arrange sturdy furniture closer together to encourage cruising.

❀ As his balance improves, he will begin to use only one hand on the furniture for support. Eventually he becomes confident enough to make a couple of unsupported steps between any small gaps in the furniture.

✿ As his confidence grows, he relies less and less on the furniture for support, moving further and further away from it. Eventually he takes three or four unsupported steps at a time.

✿ Once he is capable of taking a few steps forward, a push-along toy can help him to learn to balance. At first he will be unable to control the speed, so it is important always to supervise him, otherwise he will tend to fall flat as the toy gets away from him.

✿ Avoid using the round type of babywalker on wheels. These are responsible for 5,000 accidents a year, and the Chartered Society of Physiotherapists claims that they may also hinder physical and mental development. The society also advises parents to avoid leaving their toddlers and children in car seats for too long, as it can delay muscle development.

✿ Once your toddler has been walking properly for about six weeks, he should be measured for his first pair of shoes by a qualified fitter. It is important to invest in shoes that are both the right length and the right width. Shoes that do not support his feet properly could cause permanent damage.

Talking

The sooner a toddler is able to communicate his needs by talking, the easier it becomes for parents to control frustration and tantrums. Children learn to talk by listening, and while it makes sense to spend lots of time talking to your toddler, it is very important that you also give him the opportunity to respond to what you are saying. Communication is a two-way process and should be fun for your toddler. Although you may not understand much of what he is saying, showing him that you are really interested in his attempts at talking will encourage him to talk even more. Talking ability varies greatly from child to child, but if you have any worries or concerns about your toddler's speech development, it is advisable to seek advice from your health visitor or doctor.

Tips to help toddlers become confident talkers

✿ Reading to your child is an excellent way of increasing his vocabulary. Try to spend at least two short quiet spells a day reading to your child, pointing at things in the pictures as you do so. Avoid other distractions, such as answering the telephone or having the television or radio playing in the background.

✿ Make sure you speak slowly and clearly so that your child is able to see your mouth movements as you pronounce the words. Keep sentences short and simple until about the end of the second year. Once your toddler is stringing three or four words together himself, you can lengthen your sentences.

✿ Do not correct your toddler when he pronounces a word incorrectly as this will only discourage his attempts at talking. Instead, it is better to say the word correctly when you answer him.

✿ All toddlers love to mimic adults, so singing nursery rhymes that involve lots of actions and exaggerated facial expressions, along with the constant repetition of certain words, is a great way to help your toddler's verbal skills.

✿ Discuss things you are doing with your toddler, and emphasise the key words in your sentence. Avoid using pronouns, such as 'your' or 'it', and say instead, for example, 'Let's put on Jack's red shoes' or 'Where's Jack's blue ball?'

✿ It is worth making a list of any new words you notice your toddler using, and making sure that they are introduced as much as possible into conversations you and the rest of the family have with him.

✿ Finally, as your toddler's vocabulary increases, be prepared to repeat yourself over and over again as he constantly asks the same questions. This is all part of your child learning how to talk, and the more patient you are when answering his questions, the more eager he will be to communicate.

Dressing

By the age of 14 months, most toddlers have learnt how to pull off their hat and socks. This is an excellent time to introduce activity toys that will help your toddler develop his manipulation skills. Shape-sorter toys, and dolls that have a variety of fastenings, such as zips, toggles and buttons, will all help him to do this. It is important to allow extra time once your toddler is learning this skill. He will need lots of encouragement, and will quickly sense if you are in a hurry and becoming impatient.

✿ Between 18 and 24 months the majority of toddlers will be able to remove most of their clothes, and by 30 months most are capable of getting totally undressed and dressed, but will need help with buttons, poppers and braces.

✿ Your toddler will be less likely to get frustrated or bored if you teach him to undress and dress in stages. Once he is capable of taking off his socks and trousers, encourage him to take off another item, such as his pants, and later his top, then his vest. Use the same approach when teaching him how to dress himself.

* Encourage his independence by allowing him to choose which clothes he wears, but do limit his choice so that you remain in control.

Feeding

A toddler who is still drinking from a bottle and continues to be given lots of puréed and mashed foods during the second year will be much slower at learning to self-feed. To help develop the pincer grip (forefinger and thumb grasp) necessary for confident self-feeding it is essential to introduce lots of finger foods and chopped fruit and vegetables. Feeding bottles should be abandoned by the age of one year, and, apart from breast-feeds, all drinks should be given from a non-spill type of beaker.

* Between 12 and 15 months most toddlers will attempt to use a spoon, although they will need help with loading it and directing it into their mouth.

* By 18 months a toddler who has had enough practice will manage to eat most of his meal by himself using a spoon. Self-feeding with a spoon will be made easier for a toddler if the food is in a bowl.

* At two years of age a toddler should have developed enough

hand-eye coordination to eat his food with a small fork, and should manage to eat all his meal without assistance. Toddlers will learn to use cutlery sooner if they are allowed to join in some family meals and encouraged to copy adults.

HOW TO DEAL WITH DIFFICULT BEHAVIOUR

We've all seen badly-behaved children and fervently hoped that our own offspring won't turn out like that. The secret of raising well-behaved children is really quite simple: establish rules early on and make sure you stick to them.

Tantrums

During the critical stage of your toddler's development, with so many new skills to master, he is likely to get very frustrated. It is essential that social activities and sleep are carefully structured so that he doesn't become overtired; in my experience, exhausted toddlers are much more prone to having full-blown temper tantrums than those whose activities and sleep are carefully structured. Prevention is better than cure, and understanding the causes of tantrums will go a long way in helping the toddler to avoid them.

Main causes of temper tantrums

✿ The toddler has the mental capacity to understand virtually everything that is said to him, but does not yet have the verbal skills to communicate how he feels or what he really wants.

✿ His desire to become more independent will lead him to attempt physical tasks beyond his capabilities.

✿ A toddler will eat exactly the amount he needs to satisfy his hunger, but being forced to eat just one more spoonful to satisfy the parent's perception of what he needs is sure to lead to a tantrum.

✿ A child who has too many toys, watches too many videos or attends too many activity classes will cease to use his imagination and can become bored if he is not entertained the whole time. Boredom quickly turns into frustration if his demands to be entertained are not met immediately.

✿ Lengthy shopping trips with toddlers nearly always end in tears. If possible, arrange for a friend with a toddler to watch your child with her's for a couple of hours while you do your big shop. You can reciprocate the favour later.

Tips for dealing with toddlers' tantrums

❀ Think twice before saying 'no'. Overuse of the word can result in it not having the desired effect when you really mean it.

❀ Both parents should work by the same set of rules, otherwise the toddler will become confused as to what is acceptable behaviour and what is not.

❀ Patience and tolerance are needed to help your toddler when he is finding it difficult to cope. Punishment is rarely, if ever, the answer at this stage.

Distraction is one of the best methods of dealing with a tantrum. In order for it to be effective you must get your child's attention at the beginning of the tantrum, before he has worked himself up into a frenzy. The following three distractions are the ones that I have found to be the most effective:

1. The majority of toddlers love playing with water, so get your child to wash the baby's bottles or some plastic containers. If it is close to a mealtime, get him to help you wash some of his vegetables and fruit. On a warm day suggest that he help you water the garden.

2. Keep a small selection of balloons, party hats and poppers at hand, and bring them out when you see he is about to throw a wobbly. Alternatively, give him a bubble-blowing kit to play with; it can keep some children happy for ages.

3. Some parents keep a slab of ready-made pastry in their fridge and suggest a spot of baking when they notice their toddler is about to lose it. All the pounding and squeezing of the dough soon gets rid of excess frustration.

Time out is the next most popular method used by parents when distraction fails and a child is having a full-blown tantrum. Placing him in his cot with the door shut for a short period of time is a particularly effective way of dealing with a toddler who decides to throw a tantrum in front of grandparents, relatives or friends, whose well-meaning interventions usually make matters worse.

Holding time, which involves holding the toddler closely and firmly and talking to him in a soothing tone of voice until he calms down, sometimes works when distraction has failed. In my experience, this is effective only if the child has not already worked himself into a rage, if he is small and easy to grab hold of, or if he is sensitive and not very strong-willed.

Withdrawing attention is believed by some parents to be the best way of dealing with a toddler's tantrums. The strategy is simply to ignore the child and let the tantrum run its course. If necessary, go into another room so that the child realises he is no longer the centre of attention. I have occasionally seen this approach work, but it has been in families fortunate enough to have child-safe playrooms in full view of the kitchen. It may be worth trying to ignore your child, but it is important that he is not left in a situation where he could harm himself.

Aggressive behaviour

The majority of toddlers will occasionally use some form of aggressive behaviour, such as hitting, kicking, biting or scratching. In my experience, toddlers who resort to this sort of behaviour usually do so when they are feeling insecure. Some feel resentful and jealous when they suddenly find they have to share their parents' attention with a new baby, or share their toys with other children at playgroup. A toddler's aggression is intentional but not planned, and the child doesn't know why he acts as he does. Unlike tantrums, which are usually directed only at the parents, aggressive behaviour can often be directed at anyone the toddler feels is a threat. The child who gets into the habit of using aggressive behaviour as a way of asserting himself or of getting undivided attention will quickly become very unpopular with other parents and children.

Tips for dealing with aggression

✿ A toddler must learn that aggressive behaviour in any form is not acceptable, so I feel that it is foolish to deal with this problem by smacking him or, even worse, as some books suggest, 'biting him back'.

✿ If your toddler lashes out aggressively in some way, immediately take him to one side and explain simply and firmly that biting, hitting or whatever is not allowed, but avoid using words such as 'bad' or 'naughty', which will only make him feel more insecure.

✿ Reinforce his good behaviour with lots of encouragement and praise, with much emphasis on the times he plays nicely with the baby or other toddlers.

✿ Be extra vigilant when he is in group situations, and quickly divert his attention when he shows signs of frustration and irritability.

✿ A toddler should never be left alone with a baby for even a few minutes, and when they are together, they should be kept in full view.

Disobedience

I believe that much so-called disobedience and bad behaviour in young children is caused by parents sending out confusing signals. Here are my suggestions for improving your child's behaviour.

* Give your child plenty of encouragement. Limitless praise is not always the answer, but encouragement is one of the most important tactics parents can use to help their child. Always try to accentuate the positive and eliminate the negative by praising your child's strengths, not his weaknesses. Expressing how pleased you are when he behaves well and reminding him of the past times that he behaved well will do more to encourage good behaviour than reminding him of the times that he misbehaved.

* Grandparents like to indulge children with presents and special treats, but they should follow your rules regarding behaviour and manners. If not, your child will become confused and there will be conflict within the family. A happy, relaxed family environment with a clear set of rules is more likely to result in a confident, well-behaved child.

* Uncooperative behaviour is often the result of parental inconsistency regarding rules and limits. For example, changing mealtimes

and allowing later bedtimes to fit in with visitors or because Daddy is at home are bound to confuse a child under three years.

✿ Set realistic rules and limits to get your child's cooperation in important matters, such as getting ready for bed, getting dressed and holding your hand in the street. Avoid rules that involve your child sitting quietly for lengthy periods; it is unfair, for example, to expect a child under three years of age to sit quietly through lengthy adult lunches. Likewise, a child of this age can be encouraged to help tidy his toys and clothes away, but he is too young to be expected always to take the initiative himself.

✿ Parents' fear of making a scene means that children learn very quickly that they are more likely to get away with bad behaviour in public. No matter how embarrassed you feel, if your child misbehaves in a shop or restaurant or at a friend's house, it is better to deal with disobedience in public the same way as you would at home.

✿ Make sure your child has heard and understands your request properly. All too often parents shout across the room to small children that lunch or tea will be ready in five minutes, and get cross when the child, who is engrossed in playing a certain game, refuses to come when called at the forewarned time. **It is better to interrupt his play for a few minutes and get down to his**

**level so he can see the expression on your face and hear
clearly what you are saying. Ask him to repeat back to you
what it is you expect him to do in five minutes**. Sometimes
setting a kitchen timer to buzz in five minutes helps act as a
reminder. Using a star chart can also be an effective way of
encouraging cooperation and good behaviour.

✿ A child over two years old who is constantly in the buggy or car
and not getting enough exercise and fresh air is more likely to
be boisterous, noisy and mischievous around the home. All children benefit greatly from the opportunity to run in the fresh air
every day.

New baby, bad behaviour?

Before the new baby arrives you should look closely at your toddler's
routine, especially any rituals that take place in the morning and at
bedtime. Try to make changes well in advance so that your toddler
does not see the baby's arrival as the cause of the changes in his
life. For example, if he is used to sitting on your knee for his bedtime
story, try to get him used to sitting next to you instead. This will
make it possible for you to feed the baby at the same time as you
are reading him his story. Mealtimes may need to be altered slightly
to fit in with breast-feeding, as will the time of his bath.

Tips on preparing your toddler for a new baby

✿ The more skills your toddler has learnt before the baby arrives, the easier it will be for you to cope with the demands of two children. The majority of toddlers should be capable of self-feeding by 18 months and undressing themselves by 30 months. A toddler who is still dependent on you to help him with these things will get resentful if you expect him suddenly to start doing them for himself after the baby is born.

✿ Try to get your toddler used to entertaining himself for short spells while you do necessary chores. Introduce play activities, such as jigsaws, drawing, finger-painting and modelling playdough. Both boys and girls will benefit from having their own special baby doll, complete with feeding bottle, nappies, bath and Moses basket.

✿ Avoid major changes in your toddler's life immediately before or after the baby is born. It can take several weeks for a toddler to settle into nursery, so try to organise his starting date either several weeks before the birth, or several weeks after the baby has arrived. If you need his cot for the new baby, try to put him in his new bed at least two months before the baby arrives.

✿ Try to arrange for your partner and toddler to get used to having short spells alone together at the weekend. This way your toddler will not feel you are suddenly abandoning him when you have much-needed rests during the early weeks of breast-feeding.

✿ Get your toddler used to babies by inviting friends with babies to visit. Discuss how small and fragile they are, also how noisy they can be when they cry. Read books that explain about babies being born and what it's like to have a new baby in the family.

BOOSTING SELF-ESTEEM AND CONFIDENCE

The way parents help their child to approach the challenges he faces has a great influence on how successful he will be in mastering the challenge. All too often I hear parents express concern that their child is bound to be like them – frightened of heights, have no sense of balance, dislike dogs, and so forth. A child is not a carbon copy of his parents, so it is very important not to assume that your child's strengths and weaknesses will be the same as your own. Between two and three years of age a child is becoming very aware of being a separate person and is beginning to form views and opinions of his own. During the third year most parents work hard to build their child's self-esteem and encourage him to become more confident. However, a child's increasing independence can sometimes cause him to become overconfident, which can lead to disobedience. I think it is essential for parents to strike a happy balance between encouraging their child's new-found confidence and teaching him that there are certain rules to which we must all adhere.

Tips for improving your child's confidence

✿ It is very important that you allow your child time to think and answer for himself when asked a question.

✿ Always be consistent about rules and boundaries so that your child knows what his freedoms and constraints are.

✿ Try to encourage independence and skill-learning. During the third year almost all children are capable of self-feeding, undressing and, apart from buttons and zips, dressing themselves. Continuing to do these things for your child because it is quicker will do little to help his growing independence. Allow extra time at meals and in the morning and evening to guide him and encourage him to do these things for himself.

✿ When teaching new skills, it is important that you choose a time when your child is not overtired or hungry. Then, before doing it together, show him several times how it is done. Once he attempts it by himself it is important to praise him for his efforts, even if he doesn't get it quite right.

- Second children appear to learn many skills more quickly than first children, probably because they copy their elder brother or sister. An only child will benefit greatly from being given the opportunity to mix with other children at playgroups or on play dates arranged at home.

- It is important not to undermine your child's attempts at something new by comparing him with others. The length of time it takes to learn a new skill varies from child to child, and the most important thing is not how long your child takes, but that he enjoys learning it. If you are concerned about your child's development, it is better to talk to your health visitor than to worry unnecessarily.

- Learning a new skill requires a lot of concentration from a child, which can sometimes lead to frustration and anger. If, despite being shown several times, your child is still struggling with a new task, a difficult jigsaw or game, try to resist interfering or doing it for him. It is much better to defuse the situation by suggesting a rest period with a drink and a biscuit. Once he has calmed down and relaxed he will be much more likely to listen to your advice on how to tackle the task.

Going to nursery or playgroup

It is a big step in any child's life when he goes outside the comfort and security of home into a new place with lots of strangers and unusual activities.

Tips for making a happy start at nursery

✿ Children aged three still have no concept of time, so avoid talking about nursery too far in advance. When the time gets closer it is worth investing in some of the many storybooks that describe what happens when a child starts nursery.

✿ Try to accustom your child to being looked after by someone other than yourself before nursery starts so that separation does not come as too much of a shock.

✿ Arranging regular play dates with one or two other children who will be attending the same nursery school can make things easier for your child. If you do not already know any parents in the area, ask the nursery teacher if she can put you in touch with other parents who will be sending their child in the next term.

✿ Taking a child to nursery for the first time can be very emotional for some parents. Try not to let your child sense your anxiety when it comes to leaving him. The first few partings can often be made easier if you arrange with another mother to drop your children off together. Some nurseries encourage parents to stay with their children for a short period during the first week. This works for some children but not for others, and is worth discussing in advance with the nursery teacher.

✿ Children who start by attending nursery only one or two mornings a week, gradually building up the number of days, are less likely to experience nursery fatigue. A child who has cut his afternoon nap and begins to display signs of becoming very overtired by the evening may need to have a short nap introduced again on the days he attends nursery.

✿ A child who has learnt practical skills, such as dressing, undressing and self-feeding, and is completely potty trained will have a greater sense of independence and more confidence, making it easier to adapt to nursery, than a toddler who still relies on his mother to help him with these things.

✿ The first term at nursery can be both physically and mentally exhausting for a child. To ensure that your child does not suffer from nursery fatigue or become overtired at bedtime, make sure his bedtime routine starts early enough. A child between two and three years who is still having a nap in the afternoon would need to be in bed by 7.30pm, but a child who has dropped his nap altogether may need to be in bed by 7pm if he is to avoid becoming overtired. Remember, overtiredness is the main cause of bedtime battles and middle-of-the-night wakings.

✿ Make sure you spend a short time on his return from nursery discussing what has happened during the morning, and which activities he has most enjoyed. Express how proud you are of his efforts to try new activities that he doesn't seem to enjoy. It would be advisable to discuss with his teacher what you can do at home to make these activities more pleasurable.

Social skills

Equipping a child to behave in the outside world can help his sense of security, and part of this involves teaching him to take responsibility for his actions. The more he knows what is unacceptable, the easier it will be for him to learn to be polite and respectful.

Tips for teaching social skills

✿ Remember to use 'please' and 'thank you' yourself when talking to your child, then remind him to use these words himself. By the age of three he should be using them naturally and with little prompting.

* Eating with adults helps children to learn table manners. Try to make mealtimes relaxed and enjoyable, and do not try to instil too many rules at once. Work on one skill at a time.

* Teaching a child under three not to interrupt you is virtually impossible, so try to be patient and polite to your child – children learn best by example.

* Playing with other children is the best way for your child to learn about sharing and playing fair with others. Try to avoid aggressive or unruly children when your child starts participating in play around the age of three; an older child can sometimes be a good influence. Remember always to show pleasure and approval when your child shows consideration to others.

* A star chart that rewards your child with stickers can help encourage good behaviour.

Punishment

All parents at some stage must decide what punishment is appropriate for their child at times when he is deliberately disobedient. Parents who are in conflict about when and what punishment is suitable can send confusing signals that can lead to a manipulative child. A short, sharp smack might be appropriate in occasional circumstances, but in my experience, smacking regularly rarely works and it is not something I have ever resorted to. Remember, too, that all children are different, and what works for one could well fail with another. The following three tactics work in most instances.

1. Verbal warning – reserve a tone of voice for a short, clear explanation of why the behaviour must stop. Avoid words such as 'naughty', 'nasty', 'stupid', 'clumsy' or 'silly'. Don't let your verbal warnings become empty threats – follow them at once with the appropriate punishment if the bad behaviour continues.

2. Time out – a spell of solitude and quiet in his bedroom can often be the quickest way to calm a badly behaving child. Once you've decided on using time out, apply it quickly and calmly. It should give your child a chance to quieten and realise how he prefers to be with others. I would never leave a small child alone and upset for long periods – if he is hysterical, return to check on him every few minutes.

3. Withdrawal of privilege – when the child is very young, withdrawing privileges must be done immediately to have any effect. After a verbal warning, take away the cause of the bad behaviour. If deliberate bad behaviour continues, you may need to look at the causes and the punishments. Discuss any worries you have with your health visitor.

HABITS

All children form habits, from nail-biting to dawdling. In most cases it is better to distract a child than reprimand him, or to have a system of rewards. A star chart and the reward of a gold sticker can work wonders, although not in all cases. Try this as an incentive for tidying up or getting into the habit of cleaning teeth. Similarly, if a toddler knows he is going to be rewarded with a story or a biscuit, he may find it easier to overcome his bad habits.

✿ Try to look at the causes and understand why your toddler is forming a habit – it could be underlying anxiety or overtiredness.

✿ Try not to reprimand or get angry; patience and firmness are best.

✿ Be consistent – if something is unacceptable, it is always unacceptable.

✿ Use lots of positive encouragement and praise when your child does well.

Thumb-sucking

If your baby is approaching a year old and is constantly sucking his thumb during the day, the cause is probably boredom. The best way to deal with this is to encourage more physical activity, such as Tumble Tots or a swimming class. When at home, encourage more crawling and pushing of his babywalker, and remember to rotate his toys so that he doesn't get bored. Distraction is much better than disapproval. Making a fuss about thumb-sucking or constantly pulling his thumb out of his mouth rarely work, and usually make the baby or toddler more anxious, which increases his need to suck even more.

Dummies

If you decide to use a dummy for your baby, it is worth considering the following points.

* If a baby is happy and content without a dummy, there is little point in introducing one in the hope that it will avoid thumb-sucking.

* A sucky baby is one who, despite enjoying a full feed, keeps trying to get his thumb into his mouth and will fuss and fret until his sucking needs are met. Distraction and cuddling rarely satisfy

the need for extra sucking with babies under three months. If you decide to use a dummy, be selective as to when you use it.

✿ Allowing a baby to fall asleep with a dummy in his mouth can lead to very serious sleeping problems. Remove it before he falls into a deep sleep. It is better to have 10 minutes of crying in the early days than the hours it will take later on to wean an older and more dependent baby off using a dummy.

✿ Care should be taken when giving a breast-fed baby a dummy, as overuse could interfere with his desire to suck, which helps establish a good milk supply.

✿ Particular care must be taken to ensure that dummies are thoroughly washed and sterilised before being given to the baby. Poor hygiene when using a dummy can result in the baby getting thrush.

✿ The dummy should be taken away by the time the baby reaches four months, otherwise a long-term dependency may arise.

6
Safety

Most new parents give careful consideration to what they will need for the baby in terms of clothes, equipment and toys, but sometimes overlook the need for making the adult home environment suitable for babies and young children. The average house may seem safe enough, but it contains many different dangers and potential hazards for little ones. In the UK, accidental injury is the biggest cause of death in children over the age of one, and more children die of accidents than of illnesses such as meningitis. Around 2 million children a year are taken to hospital with an accidental injury, and about half of these accidents occur in the home. Fortunately, only a very small number of these are fatal, and the number of children dying from accidents has been steadily dropping over the last few years through greater awareness of hazards.

Of course, it is impossible to make a place absolutely safe, but there are many ways of reducing the risk of accidents and making your environment safer. A lot of these tips are common sense and would probably occur to you anyway in the course of bringing up your child. However, some dangers are less obvious, and it is worth being on your guard against them. Most homes can be made much safer with very little effort and with minimal expense – a lot of the safety equipment mentioned below is available from any good hardware shop. Some areas of safety involve building watchfulness and care into your everyday routine, from picking up and putting away choking hazards to keeping pan handles turned inwards on the hob when you cook. The safer your home, the more you will be able to allow your toddler to obey his natural impulses to explore and discover his surroundings.

HIGH-RISK AREAS

Sitting room and kitchen

Full of the equipment for everyday living, family rooms can be the most dangerous in the house. It is definitely worth investing in safety aids in both kitchen and sitting room: most are not expensive and can make a great difference in the hazard level of your home. No matter how vigilant you are, there will be moments when you take your eyes off your toddler for just a second and an accident can happen. The tips below will help to prevent this.

* Have the doors fitted with door-slam protectors – small clip-on or screw-on gadgets that stop the door closing completely – to prevent your toddler from trapping his fingers.

* Glass doors should be fitted with safety film. It strengthens and toughens glass, and prevents splinters if it is broken.

* Keep radiators on a low temperature so that your toddler does not burn himself should he touch them; alternatively, fit wooden radiator covers, although this can be expensive.

* All windows should be fitted with safety locks that allow the window to be opened slightly, but not far enough for your toddler to squeeze out. Never leave a toddler alone in a room with access to an open window.

* Check furniture for sharp corners and, if necessary, fit with safety covers.

* Chairs should not be positioned in places that could give your toddler access to potentially dangerous spots in the room, such as tables, shelves, window sills, wall-mounted cupboards and kitchen surfaces.

* All electrical sockets should be covered with safety covers, and cables and electrical leads kept out of reach. Cordless kettles

help reduce the risk of a child pulling a jug of boiling water over himself. Make sure these appliances are pushed well back on the kitchen surface.

✿ Don't hang towels and oven gloves over oven handles – they can provide a useful pull-up for toddlers.

✿ Lamps placed on small tables covered with tablecloths are a particular safety hazard, as a toddler who is just learning to walk could grab on to the table cover for support if he loses his balance.

✿ All low cupboards, drawers and the fridge-freezer should be fitted with childproof catches.

✿ Ensure that doors of dishwashers, washing machines and tumble-dryers are kept closed at all times, and switched off at the main when not in use.

✿ The following items should be locked away or out of reach at all times: perfume, aftershave, medicines, chemicals, household cleaning materials, batteries. Other potentially dangerous items include buttons, beads, plastic bags, coins, pens, pencils, drawing pins, paperclips and other small objects that might be swallowed. Keep them locked away.

While you want a healthy environment for your child, you will probably also want to make sure that the home is a stimulating and interesting place for him. In order not to hamper your toddler's natural curiosity and desire to explore, it is a good idea to set aside one drawer or cupboard in the sitting room and kitchen where you can store and rotate different things that your toddler can play with.

Hallway

The staircase is another potential danger and accounts for many of the injuries sustained by young children in the home. Falling causes the largest number of non-fatal injuries, and babies and young children are prone to falling from one level to another – off beds, chairs or changing tables, and, of course, down stairs. Aside from keeping alert when children are on a raised level, the safest thing to do is to fit a proper child safety gate at the top and bottom of the stairs. This reduces at a stroke the possibility of many nasty accidents. Build the tips below into your routine so that the safe way becomes the normal way of doing things.

✿ Always check that nothing has been dropped on the stairs before going up or down them.

✿ Never try to carry your toddler up the stairs in one arm and something else in the other.

✿ Toddlers are very wriggly as well as being unpredictable, so always keep one hand on the banister to support yourself.

✿ Once your toddler is capable of going up the stairs himself, teach him how to come back down safely, either step by step on his bottom, or feet first on his tummy.

✿ Never allow him to go up or down stairs unsupervised, and teach him not to turn around on the stairs or look back when going up them in case he loses his balance.

✿ Do not leave balls and toys, trikes and skateboards lying about in the hallway, and ensure that items such as umbrellas, walking sticks and golf clubs are not accessible.

Bathroom

The tragedy of most accidents is that they could have been prevented. The bathroom, with its combination of water, heat and medicine cupboard, can be particularly hazardous, so it's important to stay watchful and not let yourself get distracted while you're in the bathroom with your toddler. With calm and common sense, you'll be absolutely fine, but keep in mind the tips below for extra peace of mind.

✿ Never ever leave your toddler in the bath alone, not even for a few seconds. If you have forgotten the towel, it is better to pick your toddler out of the bath wet and wriggling and possibly screaming than risk the possibility of a serious accident occurring. Children can drown in 5cm (2in) of water, and even when secured in one of the chairs designed for the bath, so don't take anything for granted.

- ✿ Place a non-slip mat in the bottom of the bath, and cover the taps with a safety shield.

- ✿ Run cold water into the bath before adding the hot, and check the temperature before putting your child in it.

- ✿ Do not let your toddler stand up or jump around in the bath.

- ✿ Fit a childproof lock on the lid of the loo seat to prevent your child from lifting it and getting his fingers jammed, or even falling into it.

- ✿ Remove all medicines and cleaning fluids from the bathroom, and ensure that bubble bath, soaps, shampoos, lotions and talcum powder are out of reach or in a secure cupboard.

- ✿ Make sure heated towel rails are not scalding hot, or else mounted out of reach.

- ✿ Keep shaving razors well away from little fingers.

Nursery

Once your toddler transfers from a cot to a bed, it is important to ensure that his room is a totally safe place to be, particularly as most of the time he spends there will be on his own and he will easily be able to get out of bed to look around and amuse himself. Keeping a basic regime of tidiness will help.

❀ Continue to use a baby listener to monitor your toddler until he is at least three years of age.

❀ The cot or bed should be placed well away from the window, even if it's fitted with window locks. It should also be away from radiators: I heard of a toddler who died when he fell out of bed and got jammed between it and the warm radiator. Keep the bed generally clear of obstructions.

❀ All bedroom furniture and bedding must be flameproof. Modern furniture will reach required safety standards, but old or antique furniture may not. In the latter case you could use some non-chemical flameproofing methods.

❀ Avoid having electrical flexes and cables trailing along the floor. Battery-powered lamps may be safer alternatives for children's bedrooms.

- Chests of drawers and bookcases can be a hazard if the toddler attempts to climb up them and they tip forward. They should be secured to the wall, and drawers or cupboards fitted with safety locks so that climbing can be prevented.

HIGH-RISK ACTIVITIES

Car travel

✿ Your toddler should always be strapped securely into a properly-fitted safety seat while travelling in the car.

✿ Never allow your toddler to be held by anyone in the car, no matter how short the journey is.

✿ Unless an adult is sitting next to him in the back seat, a toddler should not be allowed to eat or drink during the journey.

✿ If a child is screaming for a drink or snack, it is better to stop the car for a few minutes than risk him choking on his food or drink, particularly if you have to brake hard.

Cooking and cleaning

We take precautions, such as wearing aprons, rubber gloves or oven mitts, when cleaning and cooking, so it makes sense to look out for young children who have yet to learn the dangers inherent in a hot kitchen or an under-sink cupboard.

✿ Make sure that pan handles are turned inwards from the front of the hob while you're cooking.

✿ If you have a low-level oven, make sure your toddler does not go near it until it has cooled down after cooking.

✿ When stacking the dishwasher, ensure that all knives and sharp-edged utensils are placed downwards in the cutlery holder, and that the door always remains firmly closed.

✿ Don't empty the dishwasher when the plates and cutlery are still very hot.

✿ When not in use, store all knives and utensils in a place where it is impossible for your toddler to get hold of them.

✿ Keep the cupboard containing cleaning fluids locked.

✿ Try to avoid having glass cupboards at a low level, and avoid keeping glassware in cupboards accessible to toddlers.

✿ Do not leave buckets or bowls of water standing around – empty them immediately. As mentioned earlier, a toddler can drown in even very shallow water.

✿ Try to avoid ironing when your toddler is around, and always put a hot iron well out of reach until it cools down.

Eating

Again, common sense is probably your best guide, but there are a few tips that might not have occurred to you.

✿ Always use the safety harness on your toddler's high chair, and attach a second set of straps so that he is secured into the chair twice.

✿ When your toddler is not in the high chair, it is important to ensure that the safety harness is not left dangling. I know of one toddler who died when he got caught up in a loose harness.

✿ Never leave your toddler unsupervised while he is in his high chair, particularly when eating.

✿ Children are prone to choking, so take special care with certain foods. Grapes, sweets and small whole pieces of dried fruit are well known as being potentially dangerous, but it was recently reported that a toddler choked to death when she tried to swallow a whole cherry tomato.

✿ Toddlers seem keen on overfilling their mouths and trying to swallow without chewing. Teach your child to take small amounts at a time and to chew properly before swallowing. This is where eating with your toddler is very important, as these are things that he can learn by role-play.

* Finally, never allow your toddler to walk or run around while eating or drinking. There could be serious consequences if he trips and falls while drinking from a beaker or eating food.

Playing inside

* Choose toys and equipment that are appropriate for your toddler's age so that he can handle them safely.

* Buy good-quality brands that meet British standards: look for the kite mark. Check the labels to ensure they contain no toxic materials or small parts that could be dangerous for toddlers.

* Broken hard toys are a potential danger, as are worn soft toys. Do regular toy and equipment checks, and clean, mend or discard any that are not safe.

* Toys are best stored in cupboards or toy boxes with lids rather than easy-to-open toy chests or baskets.

* Encourage your child to play with one or two toys at a time, then to put them away before he takes out any more. Besides encouraging tidiness, this habit will help prevent your toddler or someone else tripping over something on a crowded floor.

* A toddler playing alongside a baby should be supervised at all times. A toy suitable for a three-year-old could be dangerous to

a baby. Toddlers may want to include a baby brother or sister in their games, so make sure they're not putting the baby in any danger.

✿ Emphasise the difference between outside play and inside play, and do not allow your child to throw balls in the house or run around clutching items such as crayons, pencils or paintbrushes.

Playing outside

Young children should not be left alone and unsupervised in a garden, especially one with access to a road, an open garage or garden shed.

✿ All fences and gates should be secure, and there should be no gaps in hedges that a toddler can crawl through.

✿ Ponds and swimming pools are among the biggest dangers for young toddlers. At the very least they should be covered and fenced off, but, ideally, they should be drained and left dry until children are much older.

✿ Garden sheds and garages where chemicals, DIY tools and equipment are stored should be securely locked and the keys safely concealed.

- Do not allow pets to foul in parts of the garden where your toddler plays. Also watch out for any neighbouring cats that might be fouling your garden.

- Check that your toddler does not have access to any poisonous plants and flowers.

- Swings, slides and climbing frames should be secured firmly to the ground and safety matting laid down to prevent serious injuries.

- Sandpits should always be kept covered when not in use, and checked regularly to ensure that they are free from dirt and debris.

BASIC SAFETY IN THE HOME

Listed below are further guidelines that will help to make your home a safe, happy and relaxed environment where your child can master many of the skills he has to learn. It is important to keep things in perspective and not to impart a sense of fear or panic to your child as he goes about everyday life, so approach everything calmly and sensibly. Accidents will, of course, occur – no one could prevent them all – but it's perfectly possible to reduce the risks. A few hours spent learning mouth-to-mouth resuscitation, for example, or how to treat a burn, could make all the difference.

Fire prevention

✿ Fit smoke alarms upstairs and downstairs. Make sure they conform to British safety standards and check the batteries regularly.

✿ Have a safety blanket and small fire extinguisher in the kitchen.

✿ Ensure that all lighting is fitted with bulbs of the correct wattage. Lampshades can become fire hazards if too strong a bulb is used with them.

✿ Check all plugs are switched off and close all downstairs doors before going to bed.

✿ Never leave a toddler alone with a naked flame or with matches.

Cords and strings

✿ Kettle, iron and telephone cords are all potentially dangerous to toddlers, as are strings, ribbons and cords on mobiles, curtains and blinds. Fancy tassels and tie-backs can also present a risk. Keep all these things to a minimum, or place them out of reach.

✿ Always remove the mobile above the cot when your baby is asleep there. Once he begins to move around, stop using a mobile altogether.

Heating

✿ Central heating radiators that are uncovered should be kept at a temperature that will not burn your toddler if he touches them.

✿ It is worth investing in individual thermostatic controls on radiators so that the temperature of each room can be controlled to suit your toddler's needs.

✿ Electric, gas and coal fires should always be surrounded by a nursery fireguard that can be secured safely to the wall.

✿ Free-standing heaters should carry a BEAB mark to guarantee that they have been tested for safety. They are fitted with a thermostatic control and automatically cut off if they fall over. They should be positioned away from furniture, particularly soft-furnishings and upholstery, and never used to dry or air clothes. Ideally, they should not be used in a toddler's bedroom, but if it is necessary, they should be turned off and unplugged when the toddler is in the room alone. Remember to refit the safety cover to the socket when you unplug any electrical equipment, and to hide the safety cover when not in use.

Lighting

✿ Avoid having table lamps in your toddler's bedroom as the trailing flex is a safety hazard.

✿ Fit a dimmer switch to the ceiling light so that the brightness can be adjusted.

✿ If your toddler needs a night-light, use a small socket light that he cannot pull out. Alternatively, buy a baby monitor that incorporates a small night-light. Be sure to place the monitor out of reach, with the flex safely tucked behind a chest of drawers.

Emergencies

✿ If you have not already done so, take a course in first aid so that you are able to deal with accidents.

✿ Keep a well-stocked first-aid box in the home, and make sure that the medicine in it is up to date.

✿ It is a good idea to have a home reference book of basic symptoms and treatments for emergencies.

✿ Keep a list of emergency numbers by the phone both upstairs and downstairs, and make sure that anyone who is left to look after your toddler knows where the numbers are and also where the first-aid box is.

✿ Never leave your baby with anyone who does not understand how to administer basic first-aid.

Also available from Vermilion by Gina Ford

The prices shown above are correct at time of going to press. However, the publishers reserve the right to increase prices on covers from those previously advertised, without further notice.

FREE POSTAGE AND PACKING
Overseas customers allow £2.00 per paperback

BY PHONE: 01624 677237

BY POST: Random House Books
C/o Bookpost, PO Box 29, Douglas
Isle of Man, IM99 1BQ

BY FAX: 01624 670923

BY EMAIL: bookshop@enterprise.net

Checques (payable to Bookpost) and credit cards accepted

Prices and availability subject to change without notice.
Allow 28 days for delivery.
When placing your order, please mention if you do not wish to receive any additional information.

www.randomhouse.co.uk